# DAVID

## *A Man of Passion and Destiny*

INSIGHT FOR LIVING BIBLE STUDY GUIDE

From the Bible-teaching ministry of

# CHARLES R. SWINDOLL

INSIGHT FOR LIVING

*Insight for Living's* Bible teacher, Chuck Swindoll, has devoted his life to the clear, practical application of God's Word and His grace. A pastor at heart, Chuck has served as senior pastor to congregations in Texas, Massachusetts, and California. He currently leads Stonebriar Community Church in Frisco, Texas, but Chuck's listening audience extends far beyond a local church body. As a leading program in Christian broadcasting, *Insight for Living* airs in major Christian radio markets, through more than 2,100 outlets worldwide, in 16 languages, and to a growing webcast audience. Chuck's extensive writing ministry has also served the body of Christ worldwide, and his leadership as president and now chancellor of Dallas Theological Seminary has helped prepare and equip a new generation for ministry. Chuck and Cynthia, his partner in life and ministry, have four grown children and ten grandchildren.

Based on the outlines and transcripts of Chuck's sermons, the study guide text was written by Bryce Klabunde, a graduate of Biola University and Dallas Theological Seminary. He also wrote the Living Insights and Questions for Group Discussion sections.

**Editor in Chief:**
Cynthia Swindoll
**Study Guide Writer:**
Bryce Klabunde
**Assistant Editor:**
Wendy Peterson

**Copy Editors:**
Deborah Gibbs
Marco Salazar
Karene Wells
**Graphics System Administrator:**
Bob Haskins

# CONTENTS

# INTRODUCTION

F ew men in history have been so gifted and respected as the
sweet singer of Israel, David, the youngest son of Jesse. His
personality was a strange combination of simplicity and complexity.
As J. Oswald Sanders wrote:

> He swung between extremes, but paradoxically evi-
> denced an abiding stability. The oscillating needle
> always returned to its pole—God Himself.*

Being a man after God's own heart, David longed to serve
Him well, whether as an obscure shepherd boy along the Judean
hillsides or as the highest reigning monarch of authority. But woven
through his enviable life were tough threads of humanity, which
keep us from worshiping the man today. While great and gallant,
David was nevertheless merely a man, plagued with flaws in his
character and failure in his reign.

May these studies help us realize that devotion—not
perfection—is the secret of living a life that pleases God. We need
that reminder every day of our lives.

*Charles R. Swindoll*

Charles R. Swindoll

---

\* J. Oswald Sanders, *Robust in Faith* (Chicago, Ill.: Moody Press, 1965), p. 117.

# PUTTING TRUTH
# INTO ACTION

K nowledge apart from application falls short of God's desire for
His children. He wants us to apply what we learn so that we
will change and grow. This study guide was prepared with these
goals in mind. As you go through the following pages, we hope your
desire to discover biblical truth will grow as your understanding of
God's Word increases and that you will be encouraged to apply what
you've learned.

To assist you in your study, we've included a section called
Living Insights at the end of each lesson. These exercises will
challenge you to study further and to think of specific ways to put
your discoveries into action.

In this edition, we've added Questions for Group Discussion,
which are formulated to get your group talking about the key issues
in each lesson.

On occasion a lesson is followed by a Digging Deeper section, which gives you additional information and resources to probe
further into some issues raised in that lesson.

There are many ways to use this guide—in personal devotions,
group studies, discussions with friends and family, and Sunday school
classes. And, of course, it's an ideal study aid when you're listening
to its corresponding *Insight for Living* radio series.

To benefit most from this study guide, we would encourage you
to consider it a spiritual journal. That's why we've included space
in the **Living Insights** for recording your thoughts and discoveries.
We hope you'll return to those sections often for review and encouragement as you continue to grow in your walk with Christ.

Insight for Living

# DAVID

*A Man of Passion and Destiny*

## Chapter 1

# GOD'S HEART, GOD'S MAN, GOD'S WAYS

*Selected Scriptures*

Davia.

Jesse's youngest son. Youthful shepherd of Bethlehem. Giant-slayer. Teenage king-elect. Composer of psalms. Saul's personal musician. Jonathan's closest friend.

He rose from hunted fugitive to king of Israel. And he fell from champion in battle to aged and troubled monarch.

David—a man of glorious triumph, yet great tragedy. Uniquely gifted, but human to the core; strong in battle, but weak at home. Why are we drawn to study his life? Because David isn't a polished-marble personality. He is blood and bone and breath, sharing our struggles of spirit and soul.

Before delving into the events that sculpted the life of David— the man after God's own heart—we'll take some time to look at what's important to God's heart and how that led to David's anointing.

## A Principle worth Remembering

Since David was the only person in all Scripture whose epitaph reads "A Man after God's Own Heart," we might think of him as some kind of spiritual Superman in a world without a trace of kryptonite. But he wasn't studded with superhuman qualities. God doesn't select His servants on the basis of Atlas physiques or Einstein intellects. As Paul told the believers at Corinth:

> Simply consider your own call, brothers; not many
> of you were wise, humanly speaking, nor many mighty,
> nor many of nobility; but God has chosen the world's

1

unschooled to shame the learned; and God has chosen the weak in the world to shame the strong. God also has chosen the world's low-born and contemptibles and nobodies in order to annihilate what amounts to something, so that all humanity may be boastless in the presence of God. (1 Cor. 1:26–29 BV)

This New Testament passage echoes the Old Testament truth that resounds throughout the life of David: *God's method of choosing servants runs contrary to human reason.* That a young shepherd boy would be anointed Israel's next king made no sense in the world's mind. But in the mind of God, impressed not by brawn or brains but by a heart completely His, it made perfect sense.

## The Jews' Historical Backdrop

God's way and the world's way of selecting leaders stand in sharp contrast, like the difference in taste between a drop of honey and a twist of lemon. God's way was shown in the often sweet reign of David. And the world's way, in the bitter reign of Saul.

### The People's Choice

"The people's choice" has always been a podium for self-centered demands, ever since the day Adam and Eve passed up God's will for a bite of the forbidden fruit. Let's take a look at how Israel's choice became her curse.

*Their times.* Forty years before David assumed the throne, the period of the judges came to an end. The prophet Samuel, who was Israel's last judge, had grown old. Normally, the leadership would have been passed down to his sons; however,

[they] did not walk in his ways, but turned aside after dishonest gain and took bribes and perverted justice. (1 Sam. 8:3)

So who would be the next leader?

*Their demand.* Dissatisfied and disillusioned with God's system of judges, they decided they wanted a king. So they approached Samuel at Ramah, saying:

"Behold, you have grown old, and your sons do not walk in your ways. Now appoint a king for us to judge us like all the nations." (v. 5)

2

The other nations had heroes; Israel wanted one too—someone to ride a white horse and fight their battles, someone to protect them and look out for their interests, someone in whom they could place their trust. Someone other than God.

*Samuel's response.* The Israelites' demand pinned and needled Samuel's heart.

> The thing was displeasing in the sight of Samuel when they said, "Give us a king to judge us." (v. 6a)

A lifetime of ministering to the Israelites had produced hardly a thread of faith in them. No doubt feeling personally responsible, Samuel fell to his knees in prayer. The Lord's answer salved his sense of failure, and in His grace, He granted the Israelites' demand.

> And the Lord said to Samuel, "Listen to the voice of the people in regard to all that they say to you, for they have not rejected you, but they have rejected Me from being king over them. . . . Now then, listen to their voice; however, you shall solemnly warn them and tell them of the procedure of the king who will reign over them." (vv. 7, 9)

They would have their wish, but at the high cost of their freedom. And as the Lord predicted (see vv. 11–18), they would end up sorry they ever mentioned the word *king.*

*Saul chosen.* If Israel had been a car lot, Saul would have been Cadillac's classiest model loaded with all the extras. He was the tallest, most handsome man among them (see 9:2). Yes, Saul looked good in the Israelites' eyes. But his height and good looks couldn't hide his small and homely heart, which showed itself in selfishness, egotism, paranoia, desperation, and violence.

### The Lord's Choice

As the marks of weak character began to scar Saul's life, God began to look for a replacement. This time the new king would be His choice—a choice based not on human reason but on three essential qualifications of the heart.

*Spirituality.* God looks for those with hearts like His own. As Samuel told sinful Saul:

> "But now your kingdom shall not endure. The Lord has sought out for Himself a man after His own

3

heart, and the Lord has appointed him as ruler over His people, because you have not kept what the Lord commanded you." (13:14)

Being a person after God's own heart means living in harmony with Him, being burdened by His burdens, obeying His command to go to the right, to the left, or to stay right where you are. In a nutshell, it's having a heart that's completely His.

"For the eyes of the Lord move to and fro throughout the earth that He may strongly support those whose heart is completely His." (2 Chron. 16:9a)

When God fixes His gaze on you, does He find a heart fully committed to Him? Does He see a person who refuses to sweep sin under the carpet? A person who is grieved by wrong and intent on letting go of whatever displeases Him? Does He find a heart completely His?

*Humility.* God also looks for a heart that is humble, not swollen with pride. David learned humility while sloshing through the muck of his father's sheep pens. No one in his family seemed to notice him faithfully caring for the sheep, but God was watching. And in Jesse's boy, He saw His man to shepherd the flock of Israel.

During the long days and nights he spent caring for those smelly, stubborn sheep, David was learning what it meant to be a servant. Servants are those who are genuinely unaware of themselves—completely unconcerned about who gets the glory, what image they're projecting, or what people might say about them. The seeds of a servant's heart grow best in the fertile soil of humility.

*Integrity.* Finally, God looks for those whose lives are buttressed with the strong timbers of integrity. In David, God saw what He was looking for:

He also chose David His servant,
And took him from the sheepfolds;
From the care of the ewes with suckling lambs
    He brought him,
To shepherd Jacob His people,
And Israel His inheritance.
So he shepherded them according to the integrity
    of his heart,
And guided them with his skillful hands.
(Ps. 78:70–72)

The word *integrity* in Hebrew is rich with many synonyms—it can mean "completeness," "fulness," "innocence," "simplicity," "sound," "wholesome," or "unimpaired."[1] Physically, Saul looked down on David; but judging by the yardstick of integrity, David stood head and shoulders above Saul.

## The Lord's Method of Training

Before David was lifted to his place of honor on the throne of Israel, God had been training him. Not in the pampered schools of royalty, but right where he was.

### In Solitude

When you live in the fields tending sheep, it is solitude that nurtures you. F. B. Meyer writes:

> Nature was his nurse, his companion, his teacher.
> . . . The moorlands around Bethlehem, forming the greater part of the Judean plateau do not, however, present features of soft beauty, but are wild, gaunt, strong—character-breeding. There shepherds have always led and watched their flocks; and there David first imbibed that knowledge of natural scenery and of pastoral pursuits which colored all his after life and poetry, as the contents of the vat the dyer's hand. Such were the schools and schoolmasters of his youth.[2]

### In Obscurity

David's character wasn't formed by basking in the glow of popularity and pride. His own father paid him little attention, barely bothering to present him to Samuel (16:10–11). No, David's heart took shape away from the limelight. It was faithfulness in the little things—the unseen, unknown, unappreciated, and unapplauded—that molded David into a man who valued what God valued.

1. William Gesenius, A Hebrew and English Lexicon of the Old Testament, trans. Edward Robinson, ed. Francis Brown, S. R. Driver, Charles A. Briggs (Oxford, England: Clarendon Press, n.d.), pp. 1070–71.

2. F. B. Meyer, David: Shepherd, Psalmist, King (Fort Washington, Pa.: Christian Literature Crusade, 1977), p. 14.

### In Monotony

God allowed David to wrestle with insignificance and routine because, as J. Oswald Sanders notes, those monotonous hours watching sheep produced skills that later opened two great opportunities in his life.

> Long practice perfected his playing of the harp, and this first brought him to Saul's notice. Then he mastered the use of the sling which resulted in victory over Goliath. Many have missed God's best through a misuse of leisure.[3]

### In Reality

The classrooms of solitude, obscurity, and monotony didn't train David to be some sort of irresponsible mystic who sits on top of a hill, pops birdseed, whistles Sunday-school choruses—and when he gets a sudden wave of energy, teaches the sheep to roll over. David's training exposed him to the dangers and threats of reality: bears and lions coming to attack his flock (see 1 Sam. 17:33–37). This is why, when preparing to face all nine-and-a-half feet of Goliath's iron body, David could tell Saul with bold assurance,

> "The Lord who delivered me from the paw of the lion and from the paw of the bear, He will deliver me from the hand of this Philistine." (v. 37a)

## Two Important Truths

David didn't prove his character in that one-time battle with Goliath but day in and day out in the fields, with the lion and the bear. Before we close, let's home in on two truths we can take with us to the fields of our lives.

First, *it's in the little things that we prove ourselves capable of the big things.* Before entrusting David with the lives of the entire nation of Israel, God first gave him a flock of sheep to protect (compare Matt. 25:14–30, especially vv. 21, 23).

Second, *when God develops inner qualities, He's never in a hurry.* Although souls are saved in a mere moment, character is developed

---

3. J. Oswald Sanders, *Spiritual Manpower* (Chicago, Ill.: Moody Press, 1965), p. 115. Formerly titled *Robust in Faith.*

only with time. Giving us time to grow is part of His plan of grace (see Phil. 1:6). Just remember that no matter how much growth you have yet to do, no matter how out of place you might feel as His servant, you are—like David—chosen by God.

Remember, dear friend, that it matters not what your occupation may be, you may yet have the privilege of the kingdom. David was but a shepherd and yet he was raised to the throne, and so shall each believer be. You may be obscure and unknown, in your father's house the very least, and yet you may share a filial part in the divine heart. You may be among those who never would be mentioned except as mere units of the general census, without parts, without position; you may almost think yourself to have less than the one talent; you may conceive yourself to be a worm and no man, and like David you may say, "I was as a beast before Thee"; and yet think of this, that the marvelous election of God can stoop from the highest throne of glory to lift the beggar from the dunghill and set him among princes.[4]

### A Psalm of David

*O Lord, Thou hast searched me and known me.*
*Thou dost know when I sit down and when I rise up;*
*Thou dost understand my thought from afar.*
*Thou dost scrutinize my path and my lying down,*
*And art intimately acquainted with all my ways.*
*Even before there is a word on my tongue,*
*Behold, O Lord, Thou dost know it all.*
*Thou hast enclosed me behind and before,*
*And laid Thy hand upon me.*
*Such knowledge is too wonderful for me;*
*It is too high, I cannot attain to it.*
(Ps. 139:1–6)

4. Charles Haddon Spurgeon, *The Treasury of the Bible* (Grand Rapids, Mich.: Zondervan Publishing House, 1968), vol. 1, p. 655.

*Living Insights*

*The Phantom of the Opera. Les Miserables. Evita.* All great musicals have at least one common element—a commanding melody that weaves through the score at key moments in the drama. Sometimes it is sweetly sung by the violins; other times it rumbles in the horns. Sometimes it floats through the rafters on a soprano's voice; other times the hall resounds with its tune. You leave the theater reveling in its beauty.

In a similar way, a central, unmistakable theme weaves through David's story. As the overture plays and the curtain rises on his life, we hear it loud and clear: *God uses people whose hearts are completely devoted to Him.* W. Phillip Keller highlights this theme.

> No, God does not see as man sees. He does not measure character by charisma. He does not defer to human values. God's chief criterion for selecting special servants for mighty purposes is: *"Are you willing to do My will?"* This is the acid test. Despite all of an individual's other failings, if above all else his one consuming desire is to be *"a man after God's own heart (will),"* he will be lifted above the turmoil of his times, in great honor.[5]

What does God see in your heart? Does He see a David-like desire to serve Him? Does He see a passion to do His will above your own, an undying love for Him that sets your soul singing with praise?

At the outset of our study, why don't you take a few moments for reflection. Is your heart completely God's?

_____

_____

_____

_____

_____

5. W. Phillip Keller, *David: The Time of Saul's Tyranny* (Waco, Tex.: Word Books, 1985), vol. 1, p. 76.

In which areas of your life would you like to grow closer to God as a result of delving into David's life?

_____

_____

_____

A counterbalancing theme weaves through the drama of David's life: *God uses imperfect people*. David is as well known for his tragedies as his triumphs. Perhaps you've counted yourself out of God's plan because of past mistakes. "How can God use me?" you may wonder. David teaches that God can use us even when we've failed . . . and He will, when we give our hearts to Him.

 *Questions for Group Discussion*

1. Most people are familiar to some extent with David's life. As you flip through the mental images you've collected, what scenes come to mind?

2. The people thought Saul was the best man to be their king. On what qualities did they base their choice (see 1 Sam. 9:2; 10:20–24)?

3. What does the people's choice reveal about their motives for having a king?

4. In the lesson, we learned that God based His choice of David on his spirituality, humility, and integrity. Do those character qualities usually get us very far in the world? What does the world value?

5. Is it hard for you to stay focused on the type of character God values? Which of the three qualities do you need to develop the most and what will help?

6. Are you willing to let God train you as He trained David— through solitude, obscurity, monotony, and reality? Why?

## Chapter 2

# A NOBODY, NOBODY NOTICED

### 1 Samuel 15:24–16:13

The year 1809 was a very good year.

Of course, nobody knew it at the time. Every eye was on Napoleon as he swept across Austria like a frenzied flame in a parched wheat field. Little else seemed significant; the terror of his reign was the talk of all Europe.

But that same year, while war was being waged and history was being made, a veritable host of thinkers and statesmen were drawing their first breaths. William Gladstone was born in Liverpool. Alfred Tennyson began his life in Lincolnshire. Oliver Wendell Holmes made his first cry in Cambridge, Massachusetts. Edgar Allan Poe, in nearby Boston, began his poignant life. And in Hodgenville, Kentucky, in a rugged log cabin owned by an illiterate laborer and his wife, were heard the tiny screams of their newborn son, Abraham Lincoln.[1]

All this and more happened in 1809. But all eyes were on Austria, where Napoleon was shaping the destiny of the world. Or was he? While people focused on the present, God prepared a future. While they saw babies, He foresaw poets, prime ministers, and presidents. The "nobodies" nobody noticed were, in fact, the genesis of a new era. Their lives, their brains, their writings would dent the destiny of the entire world, long after Napoleon's fury was forgotten.

The year 1020 B.C. was also a very good year.

But not because of Saul, the king all Israel had pinned their hopes on. That year was significant because, in a secluded field in Bethlehem, God was raising up a youth named David, a "nobody" who would change Israel's course forever. Because while the people saw only a shepherd, God saw a king.

---

1. Adapted from Frank W. Boreham, "Christmas," in *2500 Best Modern Illustrations*, comp. G. B. F. Hallock (New York, N.Y.: Harper and Brothers Publishers, 1935), p. 67.

## Man Panics, God Provides

David's path from pasture to palace began with God's rejection of the people's choice: the very flawed King Saul.

### Saul's Failure

Saul struck out with God through three acts of disobedience. Strike one: He presumptuously offered a sacrifice, a duty reserved solely for the priests, when Samuel was late. Because of Saul's disregard for God's law, Samuel told him that God would take the kingdom from him and give it to "a man after his own heart" (1 Sam. 13:5–14). Strike two: He made an egotistical vow that caused his people to sin and almost cost the life of his son, Jonathan (14:24–46). And strike three: God told him to destroy the Amalekites, but rather than fulfilling the Lord's word, he spared the enemy king and the best of the livestock (15:17–11).

When Samuel came to deliver the news that Saul was *out* (vv. 12–23), Saul, who was always more concerned about his image before the people than his standing before God, wanted to conceal his failure. So he begged Samuel to return to camp and offer the sacrifice with him as if nothing were wrong (vv. 24–25). Samuel, however, replied,

> "I will not return with you; for you have rejected the word of the Lord, and the Lord has rejected you from being king over Israel." And as Samuel turned to go, Saul seized the edge of his robe, and it tore. So Samuel said to him, "The Lord has torn the kingdom of Israel from you today, and has given it to your neighbor who is better than you. And also the Glory of Israel will not lie or change His mind; for He is not a man that He should change His mind." Then he said, "I have sinned; but please honor me now before the elders of my people and before Israel, and go back with me, that I may worship the Lord your God." So Samuel went back following Saul, and Saul worshiped the Lord. (vv. 26–31)

It would be the last time the prophet stood by the king.

> Then Samuel went to Ramah, but Saul went up to his house at Gibeah of Saul. And Samuel did not see Saul again until the day of his death; for Samuel

11

grieved over Saul. And the Lord regretted that He had made Saul king over Israel. (vv. 34–35)

### Samuel's Fear

Rather than being a king who led others to God, Saul built monuments to himself (v. 12). He had no heart for God and fulfilled every bad thing God had said would happen with a king (see 8:10–18). So Samuel mourned.

When kings fail, however, no plan of God fails, and the Lord reminded Samuel of this with a gentle rebuke.

> "How long will you grieve over Saul, since I have rejected him from being king over Israel? Fill your horn with oil, and go; I will send you to Jesse the Bethlehemite, for I have selected a king for Myself among his sons." (16:1)

For Samuel, the thought of anointing a rival king—and having to pass right through Saul's town of Gibeah to do it—made him tremble in his sandals.

> But Samuel said, "How can I go? When Saul hears of it, he will kill me." And the Lord said, "Take a heifer with you, and say, 'I have come to sacrifice to the Lord.' And you shall invite Jesse to the sacrifice, and I will show you what you shall do; and you shall anoint for Me the one whom I designate to you." (vv. 2–3)

God's simple plan wouldn't raise Saul's suspicions, so, obediently,

> Samuel did what the Lord said, and came to Bethlehem. (v. 4a)

## Man Looks, God Sees

Samuel's arrival was no small matter to the people of Bethlehem.

> The elders of the city came trembling to meet him and said, "Do you come in peace?" (v. 4b)

No doubt, word of his visit had rippled through the city's streets, and the people were afraid. Had the prophet come to execute a judgment of God's? Was he bringing divine chastisement? Assuring them of his peaceful intentions, Samuel then called together Jesse and his sons to participate in a sacrifice—during which God would reveal His chosen man (v. 5).

### Parade of Candidates

The first to catch Samuel's eye was Eliab, son number one.

> Then it came about when they entered, that he looked at Eliab and thought, "Surely the Lord's anointed is before Him." But the Lord said to Samuel, "Do not look at his appearance or at the height of his stature, because I have rejected him." (vv. 6–7a)

Then came son number two.

> Then Jesse called Abinadab, and made him pass before Samuel. And he said, "Neither has the Lord chosen this one." (v. 8)

And then came son number three.

> Next Jesse made Shammah pass by. And he said, "Neither has the Lord chosen this one." (v. 9)

And the parade continued.

> Thus Jesse made seven of his sons pass before Samuel. But Samuel said to Jesse, "The Lord has not chosen these." (v. 10)

### Principle of Choice

Each of Jesse's sons looked like king material, but in God's book externals don't carry a lot of weight. God's choice is based on something much deeper—a person's heart.

> "For God sees not as man sees, for man looks at the outward appearance, but the Lord looks at the heart." (v. 7b)

How much we need to learn from God! Rather than embracing or rejecting others based on their status or lack of it, their wealth or poverty, their beauty or plainness, their cleverness or their gullibility, we should look at their character. We should look for the values they not only profess but live out. If we took the time to do this, smooth talk and charming smiles would be less likely to glaze our judgment. We need to do what Samuel did: look to the Lord

13

for discernment and wait for *His* choice, whether that's a business partner, a mate, or a leader.

## Man Forgets, God Remembers

With the parade of Jesse's sons apparently over, Samuel was puzzled. God had promised to select a king from this family, but where was he? Samuel finally asked Jesse, "Are these all the children?" (v. 11a).

### Jesse's Youngest

Jesse's oh-yeah-I-almost-forgot reply revealed that David had been overlooked.

> And he said, "There remains yet the youngest, and behold, he is tending the sheep." (v. 11b)

Why wasn't David brought in with the others? Why was he left to his job in the fields when the others were being considered for a big promotion? Jesse's attitude toward David displays two mistakes parents often make.

First, *he didn't appreciate each of his children equally.* Jesse's reply to Samuel essentially said: "Well, yes, there's David, the youngest, but he just keeps the sheep." Sadly, he saw not one of this son's kingly qualities and never intended to whistle David in from the fields.

And second, *he failed to cultivate a mutual respect among the brothers.* Jesse, like many parents, may not have been aware or ever admitted that he was favoring his older sons. But from his actions, his feelings came through loud and clear. Did the family pick up his attitude? Based on Eliab's belittling comments to David in chapter 17—you bet (see 17:28–30).

### David's Anointing

Regardless of Jesse's opinion of David, Samuel insists on seeing the young shepherd.

> Then Samuel said to Jesse, "Send and bring him; for we will not sit down until he comes here." So he sent and brought him in. Now he was ruddy, with beautiful eyes and a handsome appearance. And the Lord said, "Arise, anoint him; for this is he." Then Samuel took the horn of oil and anointed him in the midst of his brothers; and the Spirit of the Lord

came mightily upon David from that day forward.
(16:11b–13a)

Imagine David's surprise. One minute he's swatting flies in the pasture, and the next he's getting oil poured over his head and told that he'll be Israel's future king![2]

### David's Distinctiveness

After his anointing, David didn't run out to try on crowns or shine up his chariot and ride through Bethlehem announcing his new position of royalty. He didn't even bronze Samuel's horn to hang in his tent. Instead, his humility shone like the sheen of his freshly anointed head . . . as he, the king-elect, went back to the sheep fields until God's hand moved Him onto the throne.

## God Speaks, We Apply

From our study, we've seen that God rejects the self-serving and exalts the God-serving; He looks beyond the outward appearance to the heart. God notices the nobodies—who are really somebodies after all.

Let's wrap up this lesson with three applications. *First,* God's solutions are often strange and simple . . . be open. *Second,* God's provisions are usually sudden and surprising . . . be ready. And *third,* God's selections are always sovereign and sure . . . be calm.

So we leave young David where we found him, tending the sheep. Nothing has changed . . . yet everything has changed. Now when he gazes at his reflection in a pool of water, he doesn't see a "nobody" shepherd boy; he sees the person God created him to be. He sees a king.

### A Psalm of David

*The Lord is my shepherd,*
*I shall not want.*
*He makes me lie down in green pastures;*
*He leads me beside quiet waters.*
*He restores my soul;*

---

2. Jewish historian Josephus tells us that Samuel also whispered in his ear that God had chosen him to be the next king of Israel. "The Antiquities of the Jews," in *Josephus: Complete Works,* trans. William Whiston (1960; reprint, Grand Rapids, Mich.: Kregel Publications, 1978), p. 133.

He guides me in the paths of righteousness
For His name's sake.
Even though I walk through the valley of the shadow
    of death,
I fear no evil; for Thou art with me;
Thy rod and Thy staff, they comfort me.
Thou dost prepare a table before me in the presence of
    my enemies;
Thou hast anointed my head with oil;
My cup overflows.
Surely goodness and lovingkindness will follow me all
    the days of my life,
And I will dwell in the house of the Lord forever.
(Ps. 23)

 *Living Insights*

Parents, the greatest contribution you can make in the lives of your children—aside from introducing them to the Savior—is to help them see their worth. They need to know they have something unique to offer, just like every other member of the family.

That's were Jesse failed.

Do you communicate to all your children the message that they might be the ones God will choose to use in a special way? Or do you play favorites, keeping some in the field with the sheep?

Those are difficult questions. Most parents would say they try hard to value each of their children. Yet the fact remains that some children draw out our affections more than others. If we're the energetic, social type, we'll tend to favor the outgoing, bubbly child. If we enjoy music, we'll likely favor the musical child. If we run our lives by the clock, we'll probably favor the orderly, self-controlled child.

Do you see yourself favoring the child in your family who is most like you or who has qualities you admire? If so, in what ways?

_____

_____

_____

16

Do you overlook or slight the child who is least like you or who has qualities that annoy you? If so, how?

_____

_____

_____

Children are built with high-frequency emotional antennas. They hear the message in our tone of voice; they feel our emotional presence or absence in how we hold them; they notice the meaning in how we treat their brothers or sisters. They can sense who is the favorite and who isn't, even before we are aware of our own feelings.

One way to avoid playing favorites is to look at each child through God's eyes. Ask the Lord what He sees in your children. Let Him show you their hearts. Write down the unique traits that He especially values. Then write a letter to your children, sharing with each one what God has impressed on your heart.

It's not in God's plan to make us all kings. But if we will robe our children with a sense of value and crown them with the jewels of self-worth, they will, when anointed by the sweet oil of the Spirit, accomplish regal things for the King.

## _Questions for Group Discussion_

1. In your mind, flip through your high school or college yearbook. Often, the people you thought would never make it have done quite well later in life. Has anyone surprised you?

2. If Saul had been in your class, he certainly would have been voted "Most Likely to Succeed." What do you think was the central reason for his failure (see 1 Sam. 15:20–23)?

3. What does that tell you about what God values in His servants?

4. How do you evaluate people—particularly teenagers, which David was? Do you tend to measure them by externals?

5. God looks at your heart—does this fact alter the way you see yourself? Does it influence your priorities? How so?

6. Since God looks at other people's hearts, how does that affect your attitude toward them?

## Chapter 3

# SOFT MUSIC FOR A HARD HEART
## 1 Samuel 16:14–23

**E**nglish dramatist William Congreve once wrote,

> Music has charms to soothe a savage breast,
> To soften rocks, or bend a knotted oak.[1]

True words. From an infant whose hot, tear-streaked face is cooled by a mother's tender lullaby to a corporate ladder-climbing executive whose stiff deadlines are softened by the sweet strains of Tchaikovsky—music works its healing power in us all.

Music's ability to calm our tempers, soften our hard spots, and bend our rigid souls is nothing new. David, the young king-elect, besides being a faithful shepherd, was a skilled musician. And one day, God called him from the tranquil pastures to the tumultuous palace to favor the disturbed King Saul with the therapy of his music.

## Saul's Strange Malady

Saul's disorder stemmed from two actions God took against him because of his disobedience:

> Now the Spirit of the Lord departed from Saul,
> and an evil spirit from the Lord terrorized him.
> (1 Sam. 16:14)

### Departure of the Lord's Spirit

When God's Spirit departed, Saul was left with the terrible vacuum of His absence.[2] It would have been better if he had never

---

1. William Congreve, as quoted in *Bartlett's Familiar Quotations*, 15th ed., rev. and enl., ed. Emily Morison Beck (Boston, Mass.: Little, Brown and Co., 1980), p. 324.

2. References to the Spirit departing from a believer are found only in the Old Testament. For example, God's Spirit left Samson after he told Delilah the secret of his strength (Judg. 16:15–20). David prayed that the Spirit might not leave him after his sinful encounter with Bathsheba (Ps. 51:11)—a type of prayer never found in the New Testament.

known the Spirit's presence than to have savored His cup and lost it forever.

Many believers shudder when they read this passage. They wonder, "Will God take His Spirit from me if I fall into disobedience?" The answer is a reassuring no.

The Holy Spirit's ministry has changed since Old Testament days. Back then, the Spirit would temporarily empower certain people for special tasks (see Judg. 3:10; 6:34; 11:29; 13:25). Sometimes, He would indwell believers (see Num. 27:18), but rarely would He set up permanent residence within their lives. Jesus promised, however, that there would come a day when the Holy Spirit would indwell all believers forever (see John 14:16–17). That day came at Pentecost.

Pentecost marked the beginning of a new era in the Holy Spirit's ministry. Today, when we trust Christ as our Savior, the Spirit baptizes us into Christ (1 Cor. 12:13); He seals us "for the day of redemption" (Eph. 4:30); He enables us with spiritual gifts to serve each other (1 Cor. 12:7); and He indwells us as His temple (6:19).[3] In short, He lives permanently within us; and although we may choose to quench His power (see 1 Thess. 5:19), He will never depart from us as He did Saul.

### Terror of an Evil Spirit

God doubled the judgment on Saul by not only taking away His Holy Spirit but also by allowing an evil spirit to terrorize him. In Hebrew, the word *terrorize* carries the idea of falling upon, startling, or overwhelming. In a sense, it was the Holy Spirit's ministry in reverse. Where God's Spirit came to enrich and empower Saul, the evil spirit came to destroy and demoralize him.

Old Testament commentators Keil and Delitzsch make it clear that Saul's plight

> was not merely an inward feeling of depression at the rejection announced to him, which grew into melancholy, and occasionally broke out in passing fits of insanity, but a higher evil power, which took possession of him, and not only deprived him of his peace of mind, but stirred up the feelings, ideas,

---

3. For a helpful discussion on the Holy Spirit's ministry, see *The Holy Spirit*, Charles Caldwell Ryrie (Chicago, Ill.: Moody Press, 1965).

imagination, and thoughts of his soul to such an extent that at times it drove him even into madness.[4]

That Saul was being terrorized by an evil spirit was no secret to anyone within earshot of his chambers. His own servants diagnosed the problem:

> "Behold now, an evil spirit from God is terrorizing you." (1 Sam. 16:15)

Not only could Saul's servants sense the demonic presence, they knew it was "from God." But how could God send an evil spirit? Gleason Archer, in his *Encyclopedia of Bible Difficulties*, guides our understanding.

> By [his] successive acts of rebellion against the will and law of God, King Saul left himself wide open to satanic influence—just as Judas Iscariot did after he had determined to betray the Lord Jesus (cf. John 13:2).
>
> Insofar as God has established the spiritual laws of cause and effect, it is accurate to say that Saul's disobedience cut him off from the guidance and communion of the Holy Spirit that he had formerly enjoyed and left him a prey to a malign spirit of depression and intense jealousy that drove him increasingly to irrational paranoia. Although he was doubtless acting as an agent of Satan, Saul's evil bent was by the permission and plan of God. We must realize that in the last analysis all penal consequences for sin come from God, as the Author of the moral law and the one who always does what is right (Gen. 18:25).[5]

## David's Unique Ability

Tormented by an evil spirit, Saul's "savage breast" needed soothing. When Saul's servants identified his malady, they also prescribed music as the cure.

---

4. C. F. Keil and F. Delitzsch, *Commentary on the Old Testament in Ten Volumes* (reprint; Grand Rapids, Mich.: William B. Eerdmans Publishing Co., 1976), vol. 2, p. 170.

5. Gleason L. Archer, *Encyclopedia of Bible Difficulties* (Grand Rapids, Mich.: Zondervan Publishing House, 1982), pp. 179–80.

"Let our lord now command your servants who are before you. Let them seek a man who is a skillful player on the harp;[6] and it shall come about when the evil spirit from God is on you, that he shall play the harp with his hand, and you will be well." (1 Sam. 16:16)

### Description of David's Qualifications and Skills

Desperate, Saul agreed to the suggested prescription without hesitation.

So Saul said to his servants, "Provide for me now a man who can play well, and bring him to me." (v. 17)

David's name was the first to come to one of the servants' minds.

Then one of the young men answered and said, "Behold, I have seen a son of Jesse the Bethlehemite who is a skillful musician, a mighty man of valor, a warrior, one prudent in speech, and a handsome man; and the Lord is with him." (v. 18)

In the next chapter, we'll learn of a time when David fought off a lion and a bear to protect his father's flock (17:34–35). But apparently, Saul's servant had already known something of David's courage and character to give this glowing recommendation.

Isn't it beautiful how God sends people across our paths who later open doors for us in ways we never imagined? This unknown servant had just "happened" to meet David and hear him play his instrument. And God moved the king-in-waiting where He needed to be—into the palace to learn palace ways.

### Invitation to the Palace

Impressed by David's credentials, Saul sent for the young shepherd.

So Saul sent messengers to Jesse, and said, "Send me your son David who is with the flock." And Jesse

6. David's instrument was called a *kinnor* in Hebrew. Although translated "harp" in 1 Samuel 16:16, a *kinnor* was actually a lyre. Strings were "stretched across a sounding board over a blank space and attached to a crossbar. The performer apparently drew a plectrum across the strings with his right hand and deadened the strings with his left." The Greeks called it a *kithara*, from which our word *guitar* is derived. Merrill F. Unger, "Music," in *The New Unger's Bible Dictionary*, rev. ed., ed. R. K. Harrison, Howard F. Vos, and Cyril J. Barber (Chicago, Ill.: Moody Press, 1988), p. 894.

took a donkey loaded with bread and a jug of wine and a young goat, and sent them to Saul by David his son. (16:19–20)

### Position with the King

Enter the next ruler of Israel . . . leading a loaded donkey with a jug of homemade wine swinging from its side. Young David looked more like a country yokel than a king-elect. He had no inkling of protocol, no court savvy, and no understanding of political pressures; but it didn't take long for David to make a place for himself in Saul's court—and in his heart.

> Then David came to Saul and attended him, and Saul loved him greatly; and he became his armor bearer. And Saul sent to Jesse, saying, "Let David now stand before me; for he has found favor in my sight." (vv. 21–22)

Although he was Saul's successor, David didn't try to elbow him off the throne. Once a faithful shepherd, he was now a faithful servant, humble and supportive, willing to use his gifts for the king's good.

## Music's Effective Ministry

> So it came about whenever the evil spirit from God came to Saul, David would take the harp and play it with his hand; and Saul would be refreshed and be well, and the evil spirit would depart from him. (v. 23)

*The Berkeley Version* says that David's music "eased Saul." It created space in Saul's soul, allowing relief from the demon's constricting and oppressive presence. Through David's voice and the gentle strum of his lyre, the Holy Spirit chased away the tormenting spirit. In this way, young David provided a respite for the tortured king.

## A Concluding Thought

What kind of music flows from your life? Does it consist of the discordant tones of bitterness, selfish ambition, and pride? Or do people hear the soothing harmonies of God's Spirit—love, joy, peace, patience, kindness, goodness, faithfulness, gentleness, and self-control (see Gal. 5:22–23)? In a quiet moment, listen to your heart. What kind of music do you hear?

## A Psalm of David

*My heart is steadfast, O God;*
*I will sing, I will sing praises, even with my soul.*
*Awake, harp and lyre;*
*I will awaken the dawn!*
*I will give thanks to Thee, O Lord, among the peoples;*
*And I will sing praises to Thee among the nations.*
*For Thy lovingkindness is great above the heavens;*
*And Thy truth reaches to the skies.*
*Be exalted, O God, above the heavens,*
*And Thy glory above all the earth.* (Ps. 108:1–5)

 *Living Insights*

Are you wringing your hands over your future? Perhaps you're in a job that doesn't fit well. Or you have a boss who is driving you crazy. Or you don't feel at home in your neighborhood anymore. You know that God has something more for your life, but what?

If you find yourself in unsettling circumstances like these, you can react by forcing a turn in your life—grabbing the first job that comes along, manipulating a transfer, fleeing to a different city. Or you can learn from this episode in David's life.

David knew that God had something more for him, but he refused to force his way onto the throne. At the same time, he resisted the temptation to shift into park and stagnate. Instead, he worked on what he had control over—his character and abilities—and he kept moving ahead. As a shepherd, he tended the sheep the best he could; as the king's musician, he cared for Saul the best he could. He focused on the opportunities immediately in front of him and left the road ahead with God.

What areas of your life are really out of your control?

_____

_____

_____

What areas of your life are within your control?

_____

23

How can you focus less on the former areas and develop these other areas?

_____

_____

_____

To whom did David look for encouragement during his period of waiting on the Lord? Probably his Bible heroes—Noah, Abraham, Joseph, and Moses. Each of these men of faith traveled many miles through the fog of uncertainty. So did David, and so do we.

Are you willing to wait for the Lord to reveal your future in His time and in His way?

 *Questions for Group Discussion*

1. In this passage, David meets the man he will one day replace as king. What would be going through your mind if you were David?

2. Do you ever fear that God will remove His Spirit from you and abandon you? What truths from Scripture calm your fears?

3. Although God removed His Spirit from Saul and plagued him with an evil spirit, He sent David to him as an instrument of grace. What does that tell you about God?

4. What insights do you gain from David's faithful service to the tormented Saul?

5. David could have used his invitation to the palace as an opportunity to grab the throne. Is it hard for you to wait for the Lord's timing when a seemingly exciting opportunity knocks?

6. Is there a King Saul in your life—perhaps someone in authority over you who needs the soothing grace you have to offer? How can you minister to this person?

## Chapter 4

# DAVID AND THE DWARF
## 1 Samuel 17:1–54

In 1501, an unformed block of crudely-cut marble lay untouched in an Italian cathedral workshop.

By the beginning of 1504, Michelangelo had transformed it into the towering *David*, which resides today at Florence's Galleria dell' Accademia.

In this fourteen-foot masterpiece, the sculptor has embodied

> all the passionate drama of man's inner nature. The sinews of the neck seem to tense and relax, the veins of the neck, hands, and wrists to fill, the nostrils to pinch, the belly muscles to contract and the chest to lift with the intake of breath, . . . the whole proud being to quiver like a war horse that smells the battle. But of the nature of the battle there is no indication whatever; it is eternal and in every man.[1]

Indeed, in *David* Michelangelo has made stone to breathe, not only as a symbol of humanity's inner nature but specifically of Israel's David.

Chiseled into the giant statue's stony body are some of the qualities that marked David as a man of God. The knitted brow, eyes at once liquid and fiery, powerful hands—these display David's solid-marble strength, his colossal character, his larger-than-life faith. Even the slingshot slung over his shoulder symbolizes not action but attribute—in battle the young warrior relied not upon his meager material resources but upon the abundant power of the Lord.

Nowhere was this more evident than in his showdown with Goliath. Let's join David on the battlefield . . . and see who the *real* giant was.

---

Portions of this chapter have been adapted from "The Teenager Who Whipped a Giant," in the study guide *Memorable Scenes from Old Testament Homes*, coauthored by Bryce Klabunde, from the Bible-teaching ministry of Charles R. Swindoll (Anaheim, Calif.: Insight for Living, 1992), pp. 47–55.

1. Frederick Hartt, *Michelangelo: The Complete Sculpture* (New York, N.Y.: Harry N. Abrams, Inc., Publishers, n.d.), p. 111.

## Goliath: Front and Center

The scene opens with the age-old enemies of God's people, the brutish Philistines, once again threatening Israel. This time they have planted themselves on a hilltop—within Judah's territory—overlooking the Elah valley (1 Sam. 17:1–2).

### The Battleground

This broad and fertile valley, with a stream running through the middle, is one of the strategic gateways to the hill country of Israel. As the two armies eye each other across the valley (v. 3), the Philistine ranks suddenly part and a mountain of a man steps forward.

### The Champion

> Then a champion came out from the armies of the Philistines named Goliath, from Gath, whose height was six cubits and a span. (v. 4)

To avoid an all-out battle, the Philistines have chosen a one-on-one contest of champions to decide the victor. The earth seems to shake as their champion, Goliath, strides to within shouting distance and pulls up to his full nine feet, nine inches. He is an armor-plated, fully loaded fighting machine: he wears a bronze helmet, bronze leg protectors, and a coat of mail made of bronze ringlets woven on thick fabric. The weight of his armor is about two hundred pounds, and the iron head of his oversized spear weighs twenty-five pounds. Slung over his shoulder is a bronze javelin, and strapped to his side is a mighty sword. Accompanying this hulk of a man is an armor bearer, who carries a full-sized shield to defend against arrows (vv. 5–7).

Squaring his huge shoulders, Goliath bellows up to the Israelites who are peeking over the ridge.

> "Why do you come out to draw up in battle array? Am I not the Philistine and you servants of Saul? Choose a man for yourselves and let him come down to me. If he is able to fight with me and kill me, then we will become your servants; but if I prevail against him and kill him, then you shall become our servants and serve us." Again the Philistine said, "I defy the ranks of Israel this day; give me a man that we may fight together." (vv. 8–10)

What was Israel's response?

> When Saul and all Israel heard these words of the
> Philistine, they were dismayed and greatly afraid.
> (v. 11)

## Enter: David, "The Giant"

Just as the Spirit-filled David came to rescue the Spirit-emptied
Saul in chapter 16, so we now see the faith-filled David coming to
save the cowering, faithless Saul in 17:12.

### At Home

David, Saul's comforter and armor bearer (16:21), divides his
duties between caring for his aged father's flock and serving Saul
(17:12–15). In fact, verses 15 and 16 give us an interesting "split
screen" view of events: David goes back and forth between Bethlehem and the battlefield (v. 15), while Goliath goes back and forth
every morning and evening to taunt the Israelites (v. 16).

### With the Soldiers

David's father, Jesse, is concerned about his older boys' welfare
at the battle site, so he sends his youngest son down to the Elah
valley to deliver food and check on them (vv. 17–18). Arriving at
the Israelite camp just as the soldiers are marching in battle array
to the front lines, David leaves the supplies in camp and races to
catch up with his brothers (vv. 20–22).

Suddenly, all eyes focus on the valley below. David catches his
first glimpse of Goliath, who is "coming up from the army of the
Philistines" (v. 23). No longer satisfied to beat his chest from the
valley floor, the giant apparently ascends the Israelite slope to bully
his opponents on their side. And Israel's soldiers scatter like fright-
ened sheep before a growling bear (v. 24).

David, however, sizes up this pagan giant in light of God's
righteousness and power. Years spent in the fields considering God's
vast and beautiful creation had awakened David to the majesty of
the Lord. So what is Goliath compared to Yahweh? How can he
shake his fist in God's face and expect to win?

Resolved to take action, David questions the soldiers around him:

> "What will be done for the man who kills this Phi-
> listine, and takes away the reproach from Israel? For

27

who is this uncircumcised Philistine, that he should taunt the armies of the living God?" (v. 26)

The soldiers then tell him of Saul's incentives: great riches, the king's daughter, and exemption from taxes for his family (vv. 25, 27). Generous rewards, to be sure. But they beg the question, Why didn't Saul, Israel's king and most imposing man (9:2), fight for his people (see 8:20)? With the Spirit gone, Saul was more interested in self-preservation than defending the Lord's name and His people.

David's oldest brother, Eliab, overhears David's courageous words—but rather than support him, he slaps him down verbally.

> "Why have you come down? And with whom have you left those few sheep in the wilderness? I know your insolence and the wickedness of your heart; for you have come down in order to see the battle." (17:28b)

Can you feel the slam? How true it is that as soon as you start stepping out in faith, somebody will want to put you down—often another Christian or someone in your own family. Perhaps Eliab still battled the giant of jealousy that invaded his heart when Samuel anointed David instead of him. David, however, ducks his brother's jabs: "What have I done now? Was it not just a question?" (v. 29). He's too intent on fighting the real enemy to get into a scuffle with his brother.

### Before Saul

David's hope in God beams like a ray of sunshine through the black cloud of fear that has enveloped the camp. Word reaches the king, who summons David immediately. Full of confidence—the fruit of faith—David volunteers to fight Goliath.

> "Let no man's heart fail on account of him; your servant will go and fight with this Philistine." (v. 32)

The God of Israel is the only giant David sees. Saul, however, can't see past the human plane.

> Then Saul said to David, "You are not able to go against this Philistine to fight with him; for you are but a youth while he has been a warrior from his youth." (v. 33)

Saul has forgotten what it is like to fight in the Lord's strength. But David remembers past victories and uses them to fortify his faith:

> David said to Saul, "Your servant was tending his father's sheep. When a lion or a bear came and took a lamb from the flock, I went out after him and attacked him, and rescued it from his mouth; and when he rose up against me, I seized him by his beard and struck him and killed him. Your servant has killed both the lion and the bear; and this uncircumcised Philistine will be like one of them, since he has taunted the armies of the living God. . . . The Lord who delivered me from the paw of the lion and from the paw of the bear, He will deliver me from the hand of this Philistine." (vv. 34–37a)

Convinced (and relieved not to face Goliath himself), Saul says to David, "Go, and may the Lord be with you" (v. 37b).[2] Then he suited up David the best way he knew how, with his own defenses.

> Then Saul clothed David with his garments and put a bronze helmet on his head, and he clothed him with armor. And David girded his sword over his armor and tried to walk, for he had not tested them. So David said to Saul, "I cannot go with these, for I have not tested them." And David took them off.[3] (v. 38–39)

It must have been a sight—David, a 36 regular, wearing the armor of Saul, a 52 long. And here we learn an important lesson: We can't meet our Goliaths in someone else's strength, because what works for them may not work for us. We have to be who we

---

2. It's ironic that Saul would pronounce this blessing on David, considering that the Lord had already left Saul and was with David (see 16:13–14).

3. In giving David his armor and weaponry, Saul was "desirous of giving David every advantage," according to commentator Ronald F. Youngblood. However, Saul was also good at finding advantages for himself, as Youngblood continues: "It was believed that to wear the clothing of another was to be imbued with his essence and to share his very being . . . , these latter acts were probably calculated to so bind Saul to David that Saul would be able to take credit for, or at least to share in, David's victory over the Philistine giant. In a similar way Jonathan would soon give David . . . his own 'tunic' and 'sword' (18:4) as visible tokens of his covenant love for him (18:3)." "1 Samuel," in *The Expositor's Bible Commentary*, ed. Frank E. Gaebelein (Grand Rapids, Mich.: Zondervan Publishing House, Academic and Professional Books, 1992), vol. 3, pp. 699–700.

are, which is just what David did. Armed with only his sling, some rocks, and a stick, he heads down the valley . . . alone (v. 40).

## Exit: Goliath, "The Dwarf"

Both hilltops now come alive with commotion, all eyes riveted on the two combatants on the valley floor.

### Warming Up

Equipped to battle Israel's strongest, Goliath is insulted when a shepherd boy comes trotting out to meet him:

> "Am I a dog, that you come to me with sticks?" And the Philistine cursed David by his gods. The Philistine also said to David, "Come to me, and I will give your flesh to the birds of the sky and the beasts of the field." (vv. 43–44)

### Looking Up

But David is not intimidated.

> Then David said to the Philistine, "You come to me with a sword, a spear, and a javelin, but I come to you in the name of the Lord of hosts, the God of the armies of Israel, whom you have taunted. This day the Lord will deliver you up into my hands, and I will strike you down and remove your head from you. And I will give the dead bodies of the army of the Philistines this day to the birds of the sky and the wild beasts of the earth, that all the earth may know that there is a God in Israel, and that all this assembly may know that the Lord does not deliver by sword or by spear; *for the battle is the Lord's* and He will give you into our hands." (vv. 45–47, emphasis added)

*The battle is the Lord's.* This perspective will be the hallmark of David's life. Is it yours? Are you facing a giant of your own—mistreatment, fear, discouragement, guilt? Remember, "The battle is the Lord's." Not yours. Your part is to trust His power, as David did. Because He specializes in "hopeless" situations, using the window of our weaknesses to shine through His strength and magnify His name (see 2 Cor. 12:9–10).

### Wrapping Up

David's confidence enrages Goliath, who advances on the youth. Fearlessly, David runs to within range, loads his sling, and . . . *whiz.* A perfect strike! David's fastball hits Goliath right between the eyes. "The stone sank into his forehead, so that he fell on his face to the ground" (1 Sam. 17:49b).

> Then David ran and stood over the Philistine and took his sword and drew it out of its sheath and killed him, and cut off his head with it. When the Philistines saw that their champion was dead, they fled. (v. 51)

### Mopping Up

With a shout of victory, the Israelites chase the Philistines back to their hometowns, killing as many as they can catch and plundering their camps. David carries the giant's head "to Jerusalem, but he put [Goliath's] weapons in his tent" (v. 54). They are the latest trophies for David's collection; they, like the jawbone of a certain lion and the skin of a certain bear, are mute reminders of God's faithfulness and power.

## Finale: Reminders for Today's Battles

Goliath endures as a symbol of the giants we face daily. The following reminders not only help us confront our Goliaths but, with God's strength, slay them as well.

First, *facing giants is an intimidating experience.* Even through the eyes of faith, Goliath's nine-foot frame still towered over David. Faith doesn't blind us to reality, but it does enable us to see beyond the externals as we draw on God's power.

Second, *doing battle is a lonely experience.* Your Goliaths are *your* Goliaths. In fact, they may not be gigantic to anyone else but you. The battle is for you and the Lord to fight together. Your pastor can't fight it for you, nor can your counselor or friend. They may stand behind you, but only *you* can cross the battle line.

Third, *trusting God is a stabilizing experience.* It's amazing how calm David was. It was as if he knew the outcome even before he stepped into the battle. That's the nature of true faith—"the assurance of things hoped for, the conviction of things not seen" (Heb. 11:1).

Fourth, *winning victories is a memorable experience*. Has God come through for you in the past? Hang on to those victories; write them in marble, not in sand. Then, when a greater test comes, your faith will have a solid place to stand.

### A Psalm of David

> The Lord is my light and my salvation;
> Whom shall I fear?
> The Lord is the defense of my life;
> Whom shall I dread?
> When evildoers came upon me to devour my flesh,
> My adversaries and my enemies, they stumbled and fell.
> Though a host encamp against me,
> My heart will not fear;
> Though war arise against me,
> In spite of this I shall be confident. (Ps. 27:1–3)

 *Living Insights*

When David arose that fateful morning, little did he know that he would be nose-to-kneecap with a giant that afternoon. That's one of the worst characteristics of giant-sized problems—they tend to appear when you least expect them. You arrive at work to find a pink slip on your desk. On your way to the show, a drunk driver careens across the median into your car. Changing your blouse, you notice a lump in your breast that wasn't there before. Or the phone rings— the police have arrested your teenage son for possession of drugs.

Unexpected giants. They're intimidating, overwhelming, and definitely frightening.

Unfortunately, ignoring them won't make them go away. You can try closing your eyes, but you still hear them bellowing. You can put plugs in your ears, but you still smell their bad breath. There's only one way to handle a giant—face it head-on.

What are your giants?

_____

_____

How have you dealt with them? Have you faced them in faith, like David? Run from them, like the Israelites? Tried to get somebody else to fight them, like Saul? What strategy have you followed most often?

_____

_____

Is there a certain aspect of facing your giants that may be hindering your efforts—perhaps intimidation or loneliness? Write down what you struggle with most in the battle.

_____

_____

David didn't face Goliath completely unarmed. His sling, though unconventional, was still a good weapon. What resources do you have to confront your giant?

_____

_____

_____

Perhaps you lack the one thing you need to defeat your giant — faith. Have you been fighting your battles in your own strength? Can you say with honesty, "The battle is the Lord's"? If not, what has been holding you back from trusting in God's power?

_____

_____

_____

David had resources, faith . . . and a plan. What's your battle plan? How are you going to use your resources to fight the giant?

_____

_____

_____

Before you close this chapter, pray for God's strength in the fight. He's your source for real power.

# Questions for Group Discussion

1. Your "Goliath" could be a person who is menacing you, an unexpected turn of events, a physical problem, an emotional difficulty, a fear, a trial . . . just about anything that threatens to harm you. What is your giant?

2. Goliath was Saul's worst nightmare. What weaknesses in Saul did Goliath reveal?

3. What strengths in David did Goliath reveal?

4. David's victory over the giant was a political watershed for both Saul and David. While it launched David into public favor, it spelled the beginning of the end for Saul. What does that tell you about how God can use giant-sized problems in our lives?

5. How have you dealt with your giant? In faith, like David? Or in fear, like the Israelites?

6. What past victories can you recall to give you courage to trust the Lord and face the giant in front of you now? Are there Scriptures that give you comfort or confidence of victory?

## Chapter 5

# AFTERMATH OF A GIANT-KILLING
### 1 Samuel 17:55–18:9

In our childhood memories of Bible stories, David's killing of Goliath stands out as the high-water mark of his life. And it seems that this victory inaugurated his reign as Israel's king and that he had smooth sailing from then on.

But Scripture tells a different story. While the giant-killing was David's greatest achievement up to this time, it swept him out to a sea not of blissful kingship but of tumultuous testing—and he was adrift on that sea for many years.

Before taking a look at what launched this stormy period in David's life, let's review his victory and some of the positive things it brought him.

## Review: A Giant Slain

From the moment David stepped out to face Goliath, his life changed forever. Instantly, this teenager was catapulted from nobody to national hero.

### Royal Interest

Just as David was approaching the Philistine, Saul, we learn now, had asked his military commander,

> "Abner, whose son is this young man?" And Abner said, "By your life, O king, I do not know." And the king said, "You inquire whose son the youth is." (17:55–56)

Of course, Saul knew who David was. David had been the king's musician and armor bearer (16:21–23). But Saul didn't remember David's father's name.[1] Abner's response to Saul's question reflected

---

1. Saul needed to know David's father's name for a couple of reasons. First, to keep his promise of exempting the hero's household from taxes (17:25). And second, he probably wanted David as his permanent, personal bodyguard (18:2). Anybody who could whip a giant could certainly guard a king, but such a job would require his father's permission.

the position of most people. No one knew anything about the boy. Soon, however, all that would change.

> So when David returned from killing the Philistine, Abner took him and brought him before Saul with the Philistine's head in his hand. And Saul said to him, "Whose son are you, young man?" And David answered, "I am the son of your servant Jesse the Bethlehemite." (17:57–58)

### Instant Popularity

"David, the son of Jesse"—overnight that name was on the lips of every person in Palestine.

> Now it came about when he had finished speaking to Saul, that the soul of Jonathan was knit to the soul of David, and Jonathan loved him as himself. And Saul took him that day and did not let him return to his father's house. Then Jonathan made a covenant with David because he loved him as himself. And Jonathan stripped himself of the robe that was on him and gave it to David, with his armor, including his sword and his bow and his belt. So David went out wherever Saul sent him, and prospered; and Saul set him over the men of war. And it was pleasing in the sight of all the people and also in the sight of Saul's servants.
> And it happened as they were coming, when David returned from killing the Philistine, that the women came out of all the cities of Israel, singing and dancing, to meet King Saul, with tambourines, with joy and with musical instruments. And the women sang as they played, and said,
> "Saul has slain his thousands,
> And David his ten thousands."
> (18:1–7; see also v. 16)

How would young David handle this sudden success? Most people lose their sense of balance and perspective in the thin air of their rapid rise to the top. David, however, kept a level head. Saul, in contrast, lost his head, and the Holy Spirit's absence in his life became even more glaring.

Then Saul became very angry, for this saying displeased him; and he said, "They have ascribed to David ten thousands, but to me they have ascribed thousands. Now what more can he have but the kingdom?" And Saul looked at David with suspicion from that day on. (vv. 8–9)

## Relationships: Four Different Experiences

Through these events that followed Goliath's death, God continued to mold David into His man for the throne. And He used David's relationships as tools for the sculpting.

### David under King Saul: Submission

Right after David's victory, Saul enlisted him for service, eventually promoting him to command a regiment of the army (18:2, 13). And David displayed unquestioning obedience to Saul, performing his duties wisely and faithfully. He did not brag that he was to be the new king . . . poked no disloyal jabs . . . took no presumptuous liberties . . . made no attempt to out-king Saul. No, after slinging that triumphant stone, David still clung to his humility.

David's submission to Saul is a good lesson to not push our way up life's ladder but leave the lifting to God instead. To be exalted requires only one thing of us . . . that we humble ourselves before the Lord and respect His plan and timing (see Luke 1:52; James 4:10).

### David with Jonathan: Affection

Aware of the rough waters David was about to sail, God gave him an intimate friend in Saul's son Jonathan (1 Sam. 18:1). Four qualities marked the deep friendship of these kindred spirits.

1. *A willingness to sacrifice.* Although several years older and a mighty warrior himself (see chap. 14), Jonathan didn't act superior toward David. Just the opposite, he made a lasting covenant of friendship with him, ratifying it with sacrificial tokens of his devotion: his robe, armor, sword, bow, and belt (18:3–4).

Merrill Unger gives us some background about these covenant gifts.

> A covenant of friendship . . . ratified by specific ceremonies in the presence of witnesses, state[s] that the persons covenanting will be sworn brothers for life. . . . To receive any part of the dress that had

been worn by a sovereign or his oldest son and heir was deemed the highest honor that could be conferred on a subject (cf. Esther 6:8–9). Jonathan, the king's son, gave all the material gifts. David, the poor man's son, gave only his love and respect.[2]

By giving David his robe and armor, "[Jonathan] was in effect transferring his own status as heir apparent to him."[3] He saw in David the divine blessing and kingly attributes his father had lost. So he willingly forfeited his own future to allow David free access to the throne when the time was right.

2. *A loyal defense.* Saul, however, would not be as willing to step aside. Brimming with jealousy, the king set in motion several schemes to kill David (18:10–11, 17, 25; 19:1). But Jonathan courageously defended his friend.

> Then Jonathan spoke well of David to Saul his father, and said to him, "Do not let the king sin against his servant David, since he has not sinned against you, and since his deeds have been very beneficial to you. For he took his life in his hand and struck the Philistine, and the Lord brought about a great deliverance for all Israel; you saw it and rejoiced. Why then will you sin against innocent blood, by putting David to death without a cause?" (19:4–5)

Jonathan would remain loyal to his father up to a point. The moment Saul stepped across the line and threatened his friend, Jonathan was quick to take a stand, even if it meant crossing the king. His example teaches us that a true friend is never two-faced but will always defend us out of loyalty and love.

3. *An accepting heart.* Because Saul persisted in trying to kill him, David needed to flee for his safety. Broken over having to leave his friend, David freely expressed the depth of his feelings to Jonathan.

> David rose from the south side and fell on his face to the ground, and bowed three times. And they

2. Merrill F. Unger, *Unger's Commentary on the Old Testament* (Chicago, Ill.: Moody Press, 1981), vol. 1, p. 388.

3. Ronald F. Youngblood, "1 Samuel," in *The Expositor's Bible Commentary*, ed. Frank E. Gaebelein (Grand Rapids, Mich.: Zondervan Publishing House, Academic and Professional Books, 1992), vol. 3, p. 707.

kissed each other and wept together, but David more. (20:41b)

When your heart is bruised, an intimate friend will let you weep—freely and transparently.

4. *A consistent encouragement.* When David was on the run from Saul's malicious pursuit, Jonathan went to strengthen him.

> And Jonathan, Saul's son, arose and went to David at Horesh, and encouraged him in God. Thus he said to him, "Do not be afraid, because the hand of Saul my father shall not find you, and you will be king over Israel and I will be next to you; and Saul my father knows that also." (23:16–17)

No sermon. No scriptural rebuke. Just heart-to-heart, spirit-boosting encouragement. David's friendship with Jonathan was based on a kindred spirit in God that enabled them to support each other with His love during life's low points. As such, their relationship provides us the most inspiring pictures of friendship in all the Bible.[4]

### David before the People of Israel: Exaltation

In the eyes of the people, David was a star. The people delighted in his leadership (18:5), and cheered his giant leap from the lowest rung to the highest, from raw recruit to company commander. The women even composed a song to praise their new hero:

> "Saul has slain his thousands,
> And David his ten thousands." (v. 7b)

So how did David handle his stellar success? Scripture says that David "prospered" in his new role (v. 5; see also vv. 14, 15). The Hebrew word is *sakal.* In verse 30, it is translated, "behaved himself . . . wisely," which hints at the word's deeper meaning. *Sakal* can be defined: "wisdom which brings success."[5] According to Proverbs,

---

4. The charge that David and Jonathan's relationship was homosexual is completely erroneous. The claim is usually based on a twisting of David's tribute to Jonathan after his death, "Your love to me was more wonderful than the love of women." In Hebrew, the words bear no sexual connotation. Rather, *brother* (v. 26) and *love* reflect a "treaty or covenantal relationship between two individuals" (see 20:42 and 23:18). *New Commentary on the Whole Bible,* based on the commentary by Jamieson, Faust, and Brown, gen. ed. J. D. Douglass (Wheaton, Ill.: Tyndale House Publishers, 1900), p. 390.

5. *Theological Wordbook of the Old Testament,* ed. R. Laird Harris, Gleason L. Archer, Jr., and Bruce K. Waltke (Chicago, Ill.: Moody Press, 1980), vol. 1, p. 282.

people who display this sort of wisdom restrain their speech and are teachable (10:19; 21:11). That was David. He wore his success with class and wisdom . . . for the short time he owned it.

### Saul versus David: Opposition

It was inevitable that David's rising star would ignite the brooding king's smoldering paranoia. The women's song of praise, though certainly not intended to demean Saul, was what sparked the blaze. The comparison of "thousands" and "ten thousands" was merely poetic parallelism—no one was trying to imply that David was ten times better than the king. But that's how Saul took it.

> Then Saul became very angry, for this saying displeased him; and he said, "They have ascribed to David ten thousands, but to me they have ascribed thousands. Now what more can he have but the kingdom?" (1 Sam. 18:8)

Saul's insecurity led him down a four-step staircase to self-destroying hatred. The first step was a slow-burning displeasure, followed by stomach-tightening anger, which led to anxiety about losing his kingdom. That, according to verse 9, finally gave way to full-blown contempt for David.

> And Saul looked at David with suspicion from that day on.

David had done nothing to deserve Saul's wrath. He had only killed Goliath, an act Saul himself had blessed. Yet, at the hand of the king whom he saved, David would be hurled headlong into a period of mistreatment, discouragement, and pain. It didn't seem fair. But then neither do most of the trials we must endure on the hard road to spiritual maturity.

## Relevance: Our Lives Today

Those of us in the dim aftermath of a bright victory can cling to three truths from this study.

First, *not knowing the future forces us to live one day at a time.* David had no idea that the giant-killing would bring such intense opposition from Saul. He had to live one day at a time, taking things as they came and trusting God to prove Himself faithful.

Second, *having a friend helps us face whatever comes our way.* The encouragement of a close friend makes the valleys of our lives seem less vast, less threatening, less ominous.

And third, *a positive attitude and wisdom are the best defenses against an enemy.* When you see your opposition coming, it's easy to start rolling up your mental sleeves, thinking about where to throw your first jab. But the best response to opposition is to keep your cool and let God fight your battles for you.

### A Psalm of David

> Do not fret because of evildoers,
> Be not envious toward wrongdoers.
> For they will wither quickly like the grass,
> And fade like the green herb.
> Trust in the Lord, and do good;
> Dwell in the land and cultivate faithfulness.
> Delight yourself in the Lord;
> And He will give you the desires of your heart.
> Commit your way to the Lord,
> Trust also in Him, and He will do it.
> And He will bring forth your righteousness as the light,
> And your judgment as the noonday.
> (Ps. 37:1–6)

 *Living Insights*

David's greatest foe wasn't the nine-foot-nine-inch mountain of muscle named Goliath. His most dangerous opponent was his own king—the ailing master he ministered to with his music, the ruler whose honor he risked his life to defend, the man who at one time loved him as a son.

What do you do when the enemy turns out to be your own king?

The lines blur in situations like this. Is this person your friend or foe? Should you remain loyal or fight back? The emotional distress can be agonizing. You did nothing wrong . . . (David saved Saul's life!). But now this person you supported, served, and admired is gunning for you. It's confusing. It's unfair.

Your angry "Saul" might be any authority figure you sense is attacking you: an insecure boss, a controlling pastor, a domineering parent.

Are you experiencing the pain of friendly fire? From what direction are the threats being hurled?

_____

_____

_____

As you examine Saul's reaction to David in 1 Samuel 18:6–9, can you gain any insight into your attacker's motives?

_____

_____

_____

What specific guidance do the final application points provide you in your situation?

- *Not knowing the future forces me to take one day at a time.* How can focusing on today and trusting God for the future help calm your anxiety?

_____

_____

_____

- *Having a friend helps me face whatever comes my way.* Do you have a Jonathan in whom you can confide? Someone who can really listen and provide godly counsel?

_____

_____

_____

- *Being positive and wise is the best reaction to the enemy.* Write down a few "I will" statements that reflect a positive and wise response to your enemy.

_____

_____

_____

_____

_____

_____

David felled Goliath with a frontal assault and a well-placed stone. With Saul, David chose a different strategy. He respected the Lord's anointed king and waited on God to take care of this enemy. Both approaches require the same amount of faith—just different amounts of patience.

 *Questions for Group Discussion*

1. By defeating Goliath, David had met and conquered his most fearsome foe . . . or so he thought. Little did he realize his greatest enemy would come from his own camp, King Saul. Have you ever been attacked by a person you thought was on your side?

2. Along with David's greatest enemy, this passage reveals David's greatest friend, Jonathan. Have you noticed God bringing people into your life just when you needed them? What impact did they have?

3. Jonathan's response to David's success was quite different from his father's. Take a few moments to compare Jonathan's support-ive reaction with Saul's suspicious reaction in 1 Samuel 18:1–4 and 6–9. What does the contrast teach you?

4. In your opinion, what was the single most significant character quality that Jonathan displayed, and which his father lacked?

5. Review the four qualities of deep friendship that David and Jonathan modeled. What are some practical ways you can en-rich one of your friendships with these qualities?

## Chapter 6
# EVERY CRUTCH REMOVED
### 1 Samuel 18–21

It was your first time ever to ride the ski lift—after snowplowing around the bunny slope all morning—and you felt euphoric! From your panoramic view, the sky looked swimming-pool blue and the snow blankets polar-bear white. As you rode higher and higher, the wintry wind whipped through your hair and nipped at your nose.

Then you reached the top. Your anticipation quickly turned to trepidation as you skied off the lift and faced what looked to you more like a cliff than a slope. But, knowing there was only one way down, you took a deep breath and began snaking your way cautiously through the powder.

Suddenly, you heard the whoosh of skis slicing the ice and a "Look ouuuuut!" A goggled monster, bearing a SKI TEAM decal on his cap, was coming straight at you.

Next, shivering blackness.

And now, surrounded by the smell of freshly cast plaster, you face the prospect of months on crutches.

Crutches—those wooden legs with cushioned arm pads—they will be your sole support. You will lean on them while your bones are healing, depend on them to support every feeble step you take.

Not everyone has broken a leg, yet we all have hurting places in our emotional bones. And we all need support when life's icy blasts threaten to blow us down. It's only natural, for example, to lean on a career, rest on a bank account, or rely on a loving spouse or sympathetic parents. God has graciously provided these tangible supports. However, problems arise when we trust in *them* more than *Him*. When that happens, our crutches don't speed up the healing process, they retard it. So, for our own good, God sometimes moves in and takes away all our substitutes. The process is painful, but it results in stronger emotional bones and a healing that pleases Him.

## Truth about Our Crutches

As we prepare to look at how every support in David's life fell away, let's keep in mind three truths about crutches.

### They Become Substitutes for the Lord

In the midst of our troubles, the Lord offers His mighty hand to us:

> "'Do not fear, for I am with you;
> Do not anxiously look about you, for I am your God.
> I will strengthen you, surely I will help you,
> Surely I will uphold you with My righteous right
>   hand.'" (Isa. 41:10)

Patiently, God waits for us to take His hand. We can't, though, when we cling to a crutch, letting the tangible take the place of God.

### They Keep Our Focus Horizontal

Crutches can paralyze our walk of faith, because they fix our eyes on the human plane. When this happens, our godly, vertical perspective is lost in the hazy horizon.

### They Offer Only Temporary Relief

The hand of a friend on our shoulder gives us strength . . . but only for a time. It's not long before the house is empty, the lights are out, and the reassuring voices fade into silence.

## Removal of David's Crutches

Having risen from a sheepherder to one of Israel's top commanders, David had everything to make his life secure—respect, fame, friends, prestige. He could have ridden that wave of support all the way to the throne, if not for one source of trouble. King Saul.

### Crisis Reviewed

Saul, torn between the good he once knew and the darkness consuming him, distorted the women's chants of praise about his and David's victories (1 Sam. 18:6–7). He then turned demonically violent.

> Now it came about on the next day that an evil spirit from God came mightily upon Saul, and he raved in the midst of the house, while David was playing the harp with his hand, as usual; and a spear was in Saul's hand. And Saul hurled the spear for he thought, "I will pin David to the wall." But David escaped from his presence twice. Now Saul was

afraid of David, for the Lord was with him but had departed from Saul. (vv. 10–12)

As is often the case, the person out to get us is the one most afraid of us. But why did Saul fear David, who was his most devoted subject? Saul's problem was not really with David—it was with God. F. B. Meyer notes:

> Samuel had distinctly told him that the Lord had rent the kingdom of Israel from him, and had given it to a neighbor of his that was better than himself. And, without doubt, as he saw the stripling return with Goliath's head in his hand, and as he heard the song of the Israelite women, the dread certainty suggested itself to him that this was the divinely designated king. . . . He supposed that if only he could take David's life, God's purpose would miscarry and Samuel's predictions be falsified.[1]

The more David prospered, the more Saul dreaded him (v. 15)— and the more he tried to do away with him. When he couldn't kill David himself, he put him into battles where he might be killed by the Philistines (v. 17). When that failed, Saul's next plan was to ensnare David by having him marry his younger daughter, Michal (vv. 20–21, 25). But when that plan backfired (vv. 28–29), Saul put out a contract on his life.

> Now Saul told Jonathan his son and all his servants to put David to death. (19:1a)

### Crutches Removed

Insecure Saul launched a vendetta against David, who, eventually stripped of every support in his life, remained secure in God.

1. *Crutch one: David's position.* As a result of his father's murderous directive (v. 1a), Jonathan had to walk the dangerous line between loyalty to Saul and love for David. He chose to stand for the truth and defend his friend before the king:

> "Why then will you sin against innocent blood, by putting David to death without a cause?" And Saul listened to the voice of Jonathan, and Saul vowed,

---

1. F. B. Meyer, *David: Shepherd, Psalmist, King* (Fort Washington, Pa.: Christian Literature Crusade, 1977), p. 63.

"As the Lord lives, he shall not be put to death."
(vv. 5b–6)

Unfortunately, Saul's vows held about as much water as a rusty bucket.

> When there was war again, David went out and fought with the Philistines, and defeated them with great slaughter, so that they fled before him. Now there was an evil spirit from the Lord on Saul as he was sitting in his house with his spear in his hand, and David was playing the harp with his hand. And Saul tried to pin David to the wall with the spear, but he slipped away out of Saul's presence, so that he struck the spear into the wall. And David fled and escaped that night. (vv. 8–10)

"David fled." With these words, David's life as a fugitive officially began. No longer would he be a welcome member of the court. No longer would he command Saul's army. Saul's second spear-throwing attack sent the man who had stood up to Goliath running for his life.

2. *Crutch two: David's wife.* The king next ordered a hit squad to David's home to ambush him in the morning. Sensing danger, Michal helped her husband escape through the window, and once more David "fled" (v. 12). Then Michal made up the household idol to look like a man sleeping and, in the morning, told the soldiers that David was sick, to give him more time to run (vv. 13–14).[2]

Michal's loyalty, however, proved faulty. When asked by her enraged father why she let David go, she protected herself by saying that he had threatened to kill her if she didn't help him (v. 17). Unlike her brother Jonathan, Michal shrunk away from the risks of standing for the truth. She had placed her trust in her own schemes rather than in God, and her betrayal left David even more vulnerable to Saul's fury.

3. *Crutch three: David's mentor.* David fled straight to Samuel, who had anointed him and to whom David looked for guidance. After he explained to Samuel the details of Saul's pursuit, the

---

2. "The presence of an idol in David's house is disturbing, but most likely Michal kept it on hand to improve her chances of becoming pregnant." Her superstition was in vain, for she never had children (see 2 Sam. 6:23). Walter A. Elwell, ed., *Evangelical Commentary on the Bible* (Grand Rapids, Mich.: Baker Book House, 1989), p. 206.

prophet took him to his compound, called Naioth. Saul discovered their hiding place (v. 19), but with some unusual results.

One after another, three companies of the king's messengers began prophesying in the presence of Samuel and his school of prophets. Then Saul himself did (vv. 20–24)! With the Holy Spirit's help, David had time to flee again, but he had to leave behind the security of his mentor, Samuel.

4. *Crutch four: David's friend.* From Naioth, David ran to Jonathan, his closest friend. He pleaded desperately,

> "What have I done? What is my iniquity? And what
> is my sin before your father, that he is seeking my
> life?" (20:1b)

Jonathan tried to assure David that Saul would not kill him (v. 2), but Saul's spear whizzing by his ear and the bloodhounds on his trail had convinced David otherwise (v. 3). So Jonathan told him, "Whatever you say, I will do for you" (v. 4). David urged him to find out for himself if Saul was truly bent on evil, and together they agreed on a covert method of letting David know if he was safe or not (vv. 5–13). They also made a covenant to ensure David's lovingkindness toward Jonathan's family, which showed Jonathan's willingness to step aside and support God's choice of David for the throne (vv. 14–17).

Of course, Saul was indeed bent on evil, and David was not safe. Ironically, Saul said he wanted to kill David to preserve Jonathan's dynasty; but the next moment, he hurled a spear at his own son, incensed at Jonathan's loyalty to his innocent friend (vv. 18–34). Jonathan got word to David that he needed to flee (vv. 35–39); then the two friends embraced and wept . . . and left each other (vv. 40–42). This was perhaps David's most painful loss— separation from his closest friend.

5. *Crutch five: David's self-respect.* After fleeing to Ahimelech, priest of Nob (21:1–9), David escaped to Gath, Goliath's home-town (v. 10). Saul would never look for him there. Unfortunately, the people immediately recognized him as the giant's killer.

> But the servants of Achish said to him, "Is this not
> David the king of the land? Did they not sing of this
> one as they danced, saying,
> 'Saul has slain his thousands,
> And David his ten thousands'?" (v. 11)

Some "king" David was. He had no country, no queen, no subjects, and no friends. All he had left was his self-respect, but even that was stripped away when he feigned insanity to save his skin.

> So he disguised his sanity before them, and acted insanely in their hands, and scribbled on the doors of the gate, and let his saliva run down into his beard. Then Achish said to his servants, "Behold, you see the man behaving as a madman. Why do you bring him to me? Do I lack madmen, that you have brought this one to act the madman in my presence? Shall this one come into my house?" (vv. 13–15)

From national hero to madman, David had fallen from the pinnacle of success to the depths of disgrace. Even his enemies had discarded him. Would God abandon him also? We'll have to wait until the next chapter to find out.

## Lessons in Leaning for Everyone to Learn

Two lessons stand out from David's humbling experience. First, *there is nothing wrong with leaning if you're leaning on the Lord.* We've got to lean on something or somebody; life brings too many heartbreaking experiences to go it alone. But at the deepest level, we need to be leaning on God (see Prov. 3:5; Isa. 25:4).

Second, *being stripped of all crutches is one of the most painful of life's experiences.* Like those with broken legs, those whose human supports have been removed feel incredible helplessness, loneliness, and pain. Where can we go with our fears and heartaches? In a psalm reflecting on his escape when Saul sent soldiers to his home, David points the way.

### A Psalm of David

*Deliver me from my enemies, O my God;*
*Set me securely on high away from those who rise up*
*   against me.*
*Deliver me from those who do iniquity,*
*And save me from men of bloodshed.*
*For behold, they have set an ambush for my life;*
*Fierce men launch an attack against me,*
*Not for my transgression nor for my sin, O Lord,*

*For no guilt of mine, they run and set themselves*
  *against me.*
*Arouse Thyself to help me, and see! . . .*
*But as for me, I shall sing of Thy strength;*
*Yes, I shall joyfully sing of Thy lovingkindness in the*
  *morning,*
*For Thou hast been my stronghold,*
*And a refuge in the day of my distress.*
*O my strength, I will sing praises to Thee;*
*For God is my stronghold, the God who shows me*
  *lovingkindness.* (Ps. 59:1–4; 16–17)

 ## *Living Insights*

In a matter of days, Saul had wrenched every crutch from David's hand. His position, his home, his wife, his mentor, his reputation. And if he hadn't kept running, Saul would have taken his life too. Desperately, David exclaimed to Jonathan, "There is hardly a step between me and death" (1 Sam. 20:3).

Can you identify with David's experience? Do you sometimes feel trampled under the boot of an enemy or the heel of difficult circumstances (see Ps. 56:1)? Is every day a fight for emotional survival? Describe your situation.

_____

_____

_____

Have any of your security "crutches" been kicked out from under you? What are they?

_____

_____

_____

Through the storms of David's life, there was one Rock that never crumbled. Reflect on David's confidence in the Lord:

When I am afraid,
I will put my trust in Thee.

In God, whose word I praise,
In God I have put my trust;
I shall not be afraid.
What can mere man do to me? . . .
Thou hast taken account of my wanderings;
Put my tears in Thy bottle;
Are they not in Thy book?
Then my enemies will turn back in the day when
    I call;
This I know, that God is for me.
(Ps. 56:3–4, 8–9)

When all your supports have collapsed, one source of strength always remains true—the Lord. Take a moment to put your tears in His bottle and express your fears, needs, and hope in Him.

_____

_____

_____

_____

_____

 *Questions for Group Discussion*

1. Crutches are tangible sources of earthly support that give us a sense of safety. Does the concept ring true to you? What crutches do you have in your life? Do they sometimes take the place of God?

2. Can you imagine losing everything you depend on? What do you think David was feeling as he fled from one refuge to the next, only to have them all taken away? How would this experience change you?

3. How do you think the loss of his sources of human security would help prepare David to rule his future kingdom?

4. How is God preparing you to reign with Christ in God's coming kingdom (see 2 Tim. 2:12a)?

5. What encouragement does David give you in Psalm 56?

## Chapter 7

# FOR CAVE
# DWELLERS ONLY

*1 Samuel 22:1–2; Selected Psalms*

Like a fox darting in terror from baying hounds, David ran for his life from his hunter—King Saul. First he fled to Michal, his wife; then to Samuel, his mentor; then to Jonathan, his closest friend. All the while, Saul's hot fury licked up his trail, until David grasped wildly at refuge with his enemies, the Philistines.

From being Israel's hero, who used to stride through a crowded market and feel pats on the back, David was now Israel's most wanted, ducking down back alleys and fearing stabs in the back.

Where could he go? His home was under surveillance; many in Israel knew him by sight; even the Philistines recognized him. Lonely and disillusioned, David crawled into the only hiding place he could find:

> So David departed from [Gath] and escaped to
> the cave of Adullam. (1 Sam. 22:1a)

## The Cave: How It Happened

With all the crutches in his life pulled away, David havened himself within the walls of a dark, rocky cavern. At the end of his resources, with no one else to turn to, he composed this mournful song to God.

> I cry aloud with my voice to the Lord;
> I make supplication with my voice to the Lord.
> I pour out my complaint before Him;
> I declare my trouble before Him.
> When my spirit was overwhelmed within me,
> Thou didst know my path.
> In the way where I walk
> They have hidden a trap for me.
> Look to the right and see;
> For there is no one who regards me;

There is no escape for me;
No one cares for my soul.[1] (Ps. 142:1–4)

Humanly speaking, David had little to live for. The glitter of fame and fortune had turned to dross. His life as Israel's hero had left him with nothing but a stone pillow and a heart full of turmoil.

Yet he held on to God through his despair and found refuge in Him as his only true hiding place.

> I cried out to Thee, O Lord;
> I said, "Thou art my refuge,
> My portion in the land of the living.
> Give heed to my cry,
> For I am brought very low;
> Deliver me from my persecutors,
> For they are too strong for me.
> Bring my soul out of prison,
> So that I may give thanks to Thy name;
> The righteous will surround me,
> For Thou wilt deal bountifully with me."
> (Ps. 142:5–7)

From David's example, we learn that being a person after God's own heart doesn't mean never experiencing the darkness of the cave. Rather, it means being able to trust that God's light is there and that He is the God of all hope (see Rom. 15:13).

## The Challenge: What It Involved

As David sought refuge within the cleft of the Lord's mighty mountain, God brought people to him. And with these people came a challenge and renewed courage.

### Being with Others

First, God gathered David's family around him.

> When his brothers and all his father's household heard
> of it, they went down there to him. (1 Sam. 22:1b)

These same brothers stood ahead of David to receive Samuel's anointing; now they lined up behind him, supporting him at the

---

1. The superscription of this psalm reads "Maskil of David, when he was in the cave. A Prayer." *Maskil* can mean "a teaching," which would express David's desire for all who read this heartfelt psalm to learn from his experience.

moment of his greatest need.[2] God then brought four hundred men who looked to David for leadership.

> And everyone who was in distress, and everyone who was in debt, and everyone who was discontented, gathered to him; and he became captain over them. Now there were about four hundred men with him. (v. 2)

### Seeing the Needs

The four hundred who joined David at the cave were experiencing the fallout of Saul's floundering reign. Some were staggering under great pressures and stresses, others were drowning in debt due to Saul's heavy taxation, and still others were bitter of soul—they had been wronged and mistreated. So they sought out the national hero who had been similarly abused, and David welcomed them and provided the godly leadership they needed.

### Accepting the Leadership

In David's darkest hour, God gave him a ministry of helping men like him who had been worn down by injustice. Their spirits could easily have soured, fermenting into calls for a violent revolution. But David kept his eyes on God and instilled character and direction in their lives. He trained them to be mighty warriors (see 1 Chron. 11:10–47), and their number increased from four hundred to six hundred men (1 Sam. 23:13).

## The Change: Why It Occurred

Out of his dark cave, David emerged with a greater understanding of God's mercy and His purpose for his life. How did this change from lonely desperation to God-entrusted leadership take place? Three reasons emerge from three psalms he wrote around this period, each revealing the attitudes that made change possible.

### He Hurt Enough to Admit His Need

In Psalm 142, David fell on his face before God, openly expressing

---

2. Also, it's likely, considering Saul's state of mind, that the king would have searched for David at his family's home and possibly hurt them in retaliation against David. In verse 3, we see David securing his family's safety with the king of Moab.

his cavernous fear and loneliness. Remember the rawness of his emotions? "My spirit was overwhelmed within me . . . they have hidden a trap for me . . . no one cares for my soul" (vv. 3, 4). David didn't think he would honor God by pretending everything was OK. In the same way, we're not more "spiritual" by denying our hurts and covering them up with a "praise the Lord!" smile. God can handle our real needs, and He'll help us bear them too.

### He Was Honest Enough to Cry for Help

In Psalm 57, David rose to his knees, revealing the depth of his pain—and his faith.

> Be gracious to me, O God, be gracious to me,
> For my soul takes refuge in Thee;
> And in the shadow of Thy wings I will take refuge,
> Until destruction passes by.
> I will cry to God Most High,
> To God who accomplishes all things for me.
> He will send from heaven and save me;
> He reproaches him who tramples upon me.
> God will send forth His lovingkindness and His
>     truth.
> My soul is among lions;
> I must lie among those who breathe forth fire,
> Even the sons of men, whose teeth are spears and
>     arrows,
> And their tongue a sharp sword.
> Be exalted above the heavens, O God;
> Let Thy glory be above all the earth. (vv. 1–5)

Like a declaration of dependence, this psalm captures David's trust in God's goodness and care for him, two truths that are easy to lose hold of in the midst of pain.

### He Was Humble Enough to Learn from God

Throughout his life, David had tasted God's deliverance again and again. And the memory of that taste lingered with him, even during life's lowest ebb. Shortly before fleeing to the cave of Adullam, when he feigned insanity before Achish and God mercifully delivered him, David showed his teachable spirit when he composed this psalm of praise. He had fallen on his face before God in Psalm 142, risen to his knees in Psalm 57, and here it was as if he stood to his feet with hands outstretched and open, ready to receive the goodness of God.

> I will bless the Lord at all times;
> His praise shall continually be in my mouth.
> My soul shall make its boast in the Lord;
> The humble shall hear it and rejoice.
> O magnify the Lord with me,
> And let us exalt His name together.
> I sought the Lord, and He answered me,
> And delivered me from all my fears. . . .
> This poor man cried and the Lord heard him,
> And saved him out of all his troubles.
> The angel of the Lord encamps around those who
>     fear Him,
> And rescues them.
> O taste and see that the Lord is good;
> How blessed is the man who takes refuge in Him!
> O fear the Lord, you His saints;
> For to those who fear Him, there is no want.
> The young lions do lack and suffer hunger;
> But they who seek the Lord shall not be in want of
>     any good thing. . . .
> Many are the afflictions of the righteous;
> But the Lord delivers him out of them all. . . .
> The Lord redeems the soul of His servants;
> And none of those who take refuge in Him will be
>     condemned. (Ps. 34:1–4, 6–10, 19, 22)

## The Comfort: How We Can Benefit

Most likely, you will never have to seek refuge from the sword of an angry king. But as God's child, you will need to flee from other kinds of enemies: temptations, weaknesses, people who would trample your faith.

When faced with an enemy, remember that God has a secret place for you, a place of protection, comfort, and direction for your life. There, as He did for David in the cave of Adullam, He will put a song of deliverance in your heart—if you will trust, as David did, in God's love for you.

## Song of Deliverance

*You are my hiding place*
*You shelter me from the snares of my enemies*
*And surround me with*
    *sweet songs of deliverance that*
    *balm the bitter wounds*
        *of my despair*
*I will trust in You, yes*
*I will trust in You*
*For there in Your safe and secret place*
    *You will sing over my broken spirit*
*And You will make me whole*[3]

 *Living Insights*

A "cave" may be any place of escape that offers protection from life's hostilities. When troubles pelt us like hail and the dark clouds of self-doubt, grief, or depression threaten to drench us, we run to our places of refuge. We feel safe in our caves, burrowed in the heart of a mountain and surrounded by walls of stone.

Certainly, hiding places are valuable and can provide the respite we need to face the world again. However, we complicate our troubles when we become cave dwellers, barricading the entrance to our lives and not letting anyone inside.

Are you a cave dweller sometimes? What threatening enemies usually force you into hiding?

_____

_____

_____

Where do you most often retreat?

_____

_____

_____

3. Julie Martin, based on Psalms 31:12 and 32:7.

57

Thankfully, God knows how to care for His hurting children. He reached out to the despondent Elijah with the touch of an angel and a nourishing platter of food (see 1 Kings 19:1–8). When David sobbed, "There is no escape for me; No one cares for my soul" (Ps. 142:4), the Lord nourished his wounded heart by sending his family to him.

Can you see God's merciful hand reaching out to you? Who or what has He provided to nourish you?

_____

_____

_____

Along with his family, God gave David a mission—ministering to a group of fugitives like himself. Counselors say that helping people in our same situation is one of the most healing therapies. Cancer patients find a new reason to live by reaching out to other cancer patients; alcoholics, the strength to stay sober by helping other recovering alcoholics; victims of abuse, the hope to endure by ministering to other victims of abuse.

God may not bring four hundred people to your doorstep, but He may bring a coworker, a family, or even a child. Are you willing to step out of your hiding place to embrace God's mission for you, to receive a new purpose for living?

 ## Questions for Group Discussion

1. Caves of Adullam still exist today. They're not necessarily rocky shelters in the side of a mountain but the protected places where we flee to escape life's troubles. What are some of the "caves of Adullam" that you've seen people run to?

2. What are your most comforting hiding places, and why do you go there?

3. What if David had never left his hiding place? When does a cave become a prison?

4. Do any of your places of refuge control your life?

5.  David entered his cave full of despair and emerged full of praise. How? *His true hiding place was in God.* As you read Psalm 57, pick out some of the attributes of God that make Him the safest place of refuge.

6.  David's cave became a haven for him, a place where he could pour out his heart to God and allow God to heal his wounds. We all need retreats like that, particularly when the storms of life rage and batter us. When was the last time you planned a retreat for yourself? How can you make it a meaningful experience? If you can't leave home, how could you schedule some concentrated time with the Lord?

## Chapter 8

# LIFE'S MOST SUBTLE TEMPTATION

### 1 Samuel 24

Have you ever felt the urge to take revenge? Sweet and satisfying, it hangs in tantalizing clusters from the tree of temptation. Look how low the branches bend, offering you their fruit. See how delectable revenge appears, as it glistens in the sunlight—plump, red, and moist with dew.

Your boss takes full credit for the project you slaved over. Your professor unfairly gives you a failing grade. Your business partner sets you up to bear the brunt of his shady dealings. Your so-called friend betrays a confidence and spreads lies about you. Your spouse runs off with someone else, leaving you with no income and no place to live.

And now your appetite for revenge is whetted. In your mind's eye, you imagine your persecutors suffering as you have suffered, languishing in the same pit of misery that they've shoved you into. You fantasize that they call to you for help. But why should you care? With a shrug, you turn away, casually denying them the hand that they denied you.

Ah, to savor the sweet juices of revenge!

## Hard Facts to Face about Revenge

To battle this subtle and powerful temptation, we need to understand a few facts about it.

### What We Call It

Because *revenge* is such an unpleasant word, we frequently dress it up with a couple of more acceptable terms. First, instead of saying, "I'm going to get you!" we say, "I'm just standing up for my rights." This thinking naturally leads to a second label for revenge, "justified retaliation." In our minds, settling the score becomes a moral obligation. We feel justified in taking the law into our own hands and dealing out our own justice.

### How God Feels about It

Whatever we call it, God calls it revenge. And His feelings toward it are anything but ambivalent.

> Never pay back evil for evil to anyone. Respect what is right in the sight of all men. If possible, so far as it depends on you, be at peace with all men. Never take your own revenge, beloved, but leave room for the wrath of God, for it is written, "Vengeance is Mine, I will repay," says the Lord. (Rom. 12:17–19; see also Deut. 32:35–36)

We can't make anyone live in peace with us, but we can make sure the path to peace is clear on our side. Regardless of how others respond to us, God says, "*Never* take your own revenge."[1]

### The Revenge Process

Revenge may be sweet, but it sours the soul. It starts with an *injury*—someone attacks us or steals something precious to us. Silently, we churn with anger and look for a *vulnerability*, a hole in our offender's armor through which we can thrust our knife. Then, in our *human depravity*, we strike back, wounding the other person and bringing viciousness into our own selves.

This pattern goes back to the first recorded case of revenge: Cain and Abel. God rejected Cain's sacrifice and accepted Abel's sacrifice—which Cain interpreted as an injury to himself. Cain found Abel alone in the field—Abel was vulnerable. Then Cain killed Abel—violent evidence of the Fall and our resulting depravity.

Since we are not all-seeing and all-wise, it's best to leave vengeance in the hands of our just and holy God.

## A Biblical Case Study: David and Saul

In 1 Samuel 24, David has the perfect opportunity to avenge himself against Saul. The temptation to get even was strong, especially in light of Saul's record of mistreatment in chapters 22 and 23.

---

1. God's prohibition against revenge does not mean that we shouldn't defend ourselves as individuals or as a nation. Nor does it restrict us from seeking justice through the legal system. The issue has to do with personal vendettas and taking the law into our own hands.

## The Situation

After leaving the cave of Adullam at the prophet Gad's urging, David and his band headed southeast to the forest of Hereth (1 Sam. 22:5). Saul learned where he was hiding, then he accused his court of conspiring with David. He even accused Jonathan of plotting with David to ambush him—all wild inventions of his paranoid mind (vv. 6–8).

When Saul discovered that Ahimelech the priest innocently aided David (see 21:1–9a), Saul ordered his death. Only Doeg, a pagan Edomite, was debased enough to carry out Saul's order. In cold blood, Doeg murdered Ahimelech, his family, and every man, woman, and child in Nob, the city of the priests. Total annihilation was usually reserved for Israel's worst enemies, which is what Saul considered anyone who stood in his way (22:11–19). Only one son of Ahimelech survived, Abiathar, who would become David's priest (vv. 20–23).

By killing the priests, Saul severed all ties with God and set himself adrift on a dangerous sea of rebellion. David, in contrast, rested solidly on the Lord. When he learned that the Philistines were attacking the Judean city of Keilah, he sought the Lord's direction and saved the city (23:1–5). But Saul pursued him there, and God told David that the people he had just rescued would turn him over to Saul. So David and his men escaped into the wilderness of Ziph—but Saul still "sought him every day" (vv. 6–14).

Jonathan, risking his own life, offered David a brief respite of encouragement by coming to him in the wilderness. He reassured David that he would be Israel's next king and that even Saul knew that (vv. 15–18). Jonathan's loyalty stands in stark contrast to the betrayal of the Ziphites, who went out of their way to inform Saul of David's whereabouts (vv. 19–24). Saul nearly got David in the wilderness of Maon, but word of a Philistine attack pulled Saul away. Once more, God frustrated Saul's wicked intent.

Now we find David and his men safely camouflaged in the cool caves of Engedi, temporarily out of Saul's reach. But tenacious Saul gets wind of David's position.

> Now it came about when Saul returned from pursuing the Philistines, he was told, saying, "Behold, David is in the wilderness of Engedi." Then Saul took three thousand chosen men from all Israel, and went to seek David and his men in front of the Rocks of the Wild Goats. (24:1–2)

Three thousand men? Chosen from all Israel? It's clear that Saul means business.

### The Temptation

Saul momentarily steps into a cave to "relieve himself," but little does he know that David and his men are hiding in the darkness of that same cave (v. 3). For the first time since he has injured David, Saul is vulnerable.

Once David's men see Saul's vulnerability, their human natures shift into overdrive. Their words, masked by a veil of spirituality, encourage David to retaliate.

> And the men of David said to him, "Behold, this is the day of which the Lord said to you, 'Behold; I am about to give your enemy into your hand, and you shall do to him as it seems good to you.'" (v. 4a)

When did God ever say this? Still, David can't completely give up this opportunity to get even. He wants at least a taste of the sweetness of revenge.

> Then David arose and cut off the edge of Saul's robe secretly. (v. 4b)

David barely slides his knife back into its sheath when God pricks his conscience (v. 5). Repentant, he tells his men,

> "Far be it from me because of the Lord that I should do this thing to my lord, the Lord's anointed, to stretch out my hand against him, since he is the Lord's anointed." (v. 6)

Sensitive to even the little sins—sins we often don't take seriously—David convinces his men that this approach is wrong. They all need to leave the vengeance to God.

> And David persuaded his men with these words and did not allow them to rise up against Saul.[2] And Saul arose, left the cave, and went on his way. (v. 7)

---

2. The Hebrew word for *persuaded* can be rendered "torn apart." Because of David's conviction, his men, too, were torn up about their desire to get even with Saul.

## The Conversation

Because David refuses to get even with Saul, God blesses him. The proverbs tell us,

> When a man's ways are pleasing to the Lord,
> He makes even his enemies to be at peace with him.
> (Prov. 16:7)

Let's see how God brings peace between David and Saul through their conversation in the cliffs.

*David to Saul.* When Saul leaves the cave, David follows him out to talk to him, torn garment in hand. He wants to prove both his innocence and his integrity. The conversation begins with David openly displaying his respect for Saul.

> Now afterward David arose and went out of the cave and called after Saul, saying, "My lord the king!" And when Saul looked behind him, David bowed with his face to the ground and prostrated himself. (1 Sam. 24:8)

Next, David tries to set the record straight.

> And David said to Saul, "Why do you listen to the words of men, saying, 'Behold, David seeks to harm you'?" (v. 9)

Then, to his plea for innocence, he adds verbal and physical proof.

> "Behold, this day your eyes have seen that the Lord had given you today into my hand in the cave, and some said to kill you, but my eye had pity on you; and I said, 'I will not stretch out my hand against my lord, for he is the Lord's anointed.' Now, my father, see! Indeed, see the edge of your robe in my hand! For in that I cut off the edge of your robe and did not kill you, know and perceive that there is no evil or rebellion in my hands, and I have not sinned against you, though you are lying in wait for my life to take it." (vv. 10–11)

Finally, David tells Saul he will let God judge between them (vv. 12–15). More than revenge, David desires the Lord's will to be done.

*Saul to David.* David's honest words of confrontation soften the tough-hearted Saul.

> Now it came about when David had finished speaking these words to Saul, that Saul said, "Is this your voice, my son David?" Then Saul lifted up his voice and wept. And he said to David, "You are more righteous than I; for you have dealt well with me, while I have dealt wickedly with you. And you have declared today that you have done good to me, that the Lord delivered me into your hand and yet you did not kill me. For if a man finds his enemy, will he let him go away safely? May the Lord therefore reward you with good in return for what you have done to me this day. And now, behold, I know that you shall surely be king, and that the kingdom of Israel shall be established in your hand." (vv. 16–20)

At the end of his reply, Saul makes a plea, and the two men depart in peace.

> "So now swear to me by the Lord that you will not cut off my descendants after me, and that you will not destroy my name from my father's household."[3] And David swore to Saul. And Saul went to his home, but David and his men went up to the stronghold. (vv. 21–22)

## Tough Principles to Practice

Revenge is as old as human nature. And, while not all vengeance creates a tragedy as bitter as Cain and Abel's, it all makes a travesty of God's plan for our lives. If you're plotting revenge, however small and insignificant you may think it to be, surrender it now. Release your grip on your get-even scheme, and place the control in God's hands. Let's reflect on some principles that will help us relinquish our desire for revenge.

---

3. "It was quite common in the ancient world for the first ruler of a new dynasty to secure his position by murdering all potential claimants to the throne from the preceding dynasty." J. Robert Vannoy, "1 Samuel," *The NIV Study Bible*, ed. Kenneth Barker and others (Grand Rapids, Mich.: Zondervan Publishing House, 1985), p. 406, note on 20:14. Because he knew that God would secure his position, David could extend mercy and kindness to Saul's family.

*Since humanity is depraved, expect to be mistreated.* The same human nature that beat in Saul's heart beats in all our hearts. Trouble comes when we expect, and then demand, too much from others. People are fallible; hurt feelings are par for the course.

*Since mistreatment by others is inevitable, we can anticipate our desires for revenge.* Acknowledging the urge to get even is not the same as retaliating. Rather, when we're aware of what's going on inside, we have time to feel and pray and think and then choose a course of action that reflects our trust in God.

*Since the temptation toward revenge is predictable, refuse to fight in the flesh.* We can make up our minds ahead of time to leave things in God's hands, which will make us less likely to impulsively lash back when we're wronged. We're not responsible for how others behave, but we are responsible for making sure we're not mistreating others in return.

### A Psalm of David

*Behold, God is my helper;*
*The Lord is the sustainer of my soul*
*He will recompense the evil to my foes;*
*Destroy them in Thy faithfulness.*
*Willingly I will sacrifice to Thee;*
*I will give thanks to Thy name, O Lord, for it is good.*
*For He has delivered me from all trouble;*
*And my eye has looked with satisfaction upon my*
*enemies.* (Ps. 54:4–7)

 *Living Insights*

If you catalogued all your injuries in life, imagine how long the list would be! Many of the injuries have been minor bumps and bruises that healed without a scar. Remember the time your best friend in first grade asked someone else to ride the teeter-totter? Some injuries, though, have never completely healed. A few may still be open and very tender wounds.

Has someone injured you so deeply that you still carry the wounds with you?

---

---

How have you dealt with the pain? Have you harbored fantasies of revenge?

_____

_____

_____

David resisted the temptation to sink his knife into Saul's heart, but he couldn't resist the temptation to cut off some of his robe. Have you attacked your offender like that, with a little cut here or a jab there?

Cutting Saul's robe may have felt good at the moment, but it didn't mend David's injury. Healing came when David confronted Saul with his misdeeds—not to get even but to tell the truth.

Reread what David said to Saul in 1 Samuel 24:8–15. In what ways can his example help you confront your offender?

_____

_____

_____

_____

_____

_____

Is it time for you to step out of your cave of private heartache and be honest with the person who hurt you? You may not change the other person, but you may begin to feel a sense of closure with the past. And that's the first and biggest step toward healing.

 ## Questions for Group Discussion

1. Relate an example of revenge in a book you read or a movie you saw. Did the story portray revenge in a positive or negative light? What feelings did the revenge scene stir in you?

2. If Hollywood had written the story of Saul and David, the filmmakers probably would have scripted a fight scene in which David kills the wicked King Saul, before taking his rightful place

on the throne. Sounds like a good plot to us; why would God have disapproved of it?

3. Why do you think God commands us not to take our own revenge?

4. Why was it wrong for David to cut off a piece of Saul's robe?

5. Have you tasted the sweetness of revenge, as well as its sour aftertaste? Share your experience, if you feel comfortable.

6. In what ways does David's honest confrontation with Saul give you a positive example of how to deal with someone who has injured you? If this type of confrontation isn't possible, what could you do to bring closure to the situation?

## Chapter 9

# WHAT TO FEED AN ANGRY MAN

*1 Samuel 25*

The rays of each sunrise bring new opportunities to take and new choices to make. Each day carries with it a certain aura of adventure and growth and the possibility of success. But it also brings the painful possibility of failure. Though God's mercies are new every morning, so are Satan's schemes.

> *Yesterday's victories*
> *may become today's temptations;*
> *the sin we shunned yesterday,*
> *we may embrace today.*
>
> *Sunday's unconditional love*
> *can turn to Monday's selfishness.*
>
> *A tender, forgiving heart*
> *can become punitive and tough.*
>
> *And a refusal to retaliate*
> *can turn to cold-blooded revenge.*

Like the rest of us, David learned the hard way that you can't live today on yesterday's obedience. In the last chapter, he chose to leave vengeance in God's hands; in today's scene, he is overcome by hotheaded impetuosity and nearly commits murder.

However, this story doesn't end in the shedding of blood but in an outpouring of grace. Let's take a look at David in one of his most human moments—and at the woman God used to turn his hostile heart back to Himself.

This chapter has been adapted from "The Woman Who Saved Her Husband's Neck," from the study guide *Memorable Scenes from Old Testament Homes*, coauthored by Bryce Klabunde, from the Bible-teaching ministry of Charles R. Swindoll (Anaheim, Calif.: Insight for Living, 1992), pp. 56–64.

# Background

With Saul's manhunt momentarily called off, David and his men wearily returned to their strongholds in Engedi (1 Sam. 24:22). A wary peace was in place, but relief was all too brief. Not because of any new moves from Saul; rather, Israel's last judge and pre-eminent prophet had died.

> Then Samuel died; and all Israel gathered together and mourned for him, and buried him at his house in Ramah. (25:1a)

Samuel . . . spiritual conscience of the nation, spokesman for God, anointer of kings. He anointed Saul and watched the man turn away from God and fail. He anointed David and watched him succeed and then run for his life. He never saw this young man after God's own heart ascend Israel's throne.

This chapter in David's life, then, opens with tremendous loss. Significantly, it also concludes with mention of another loss—Saul has given David's wife Michal to another man (v. 44). Encircled by pain, David must have wondered if God would ever avenge Saul's evil and uphold his righteous cause.

Tired and sad, David left the cool of Engedi to scratch out some sort of living in the wilderness of Maon.[1] There he and his men employ themselves in protecting the local ranchers and their herds from invading tribes and wild animals. Theirs is a volunteer force; no contracts are signed. But it's customary for ranchers to compensate their protectors with a small portion of the harvest and the herds.

David's rancher is Nabal, a wealthy man who has three thousand sheep and a thousand goats (v. 2). And now it is sheepshearing time—time for Nabal to collect the wool and the profits from his vast enterprise. The sheep, however, aren't the only ones to get clipped by Nabal.

## Main Characters

The story unfolds like several scenes in a one-act play. Before we reveal too much of the plot, let's meet the main characters.

---

1. Though the NASB says, "And David arose and went down to the wilderness of Paran" (v. 1b), he most likely went to Maon in Judah, as the NIV states, since that region is mentioned in verse 2. The Wilderness of Paran was much farther south, about a hundred miles or more south than the Negev—the southernmost region of Judah.

### Nabal

Although from a distinguished lineage, "a Calebite," Nabal showed none of the tenacious faith his ancestor Caleb had (see Num. 13–14; Josh. 14). Scripture says he was "harsh and evil in his dealings" (1 Sam. 25:3b). His name even means "fool"; and he recognized no authority above his own, not even God's (compare Ps. 14:1). Somehow, though, he was blessed with a wife who was everything he was not, Abigail.

### Abigail

Unlike Nabal, Abigail was intelligent—clear-thinking and wise. Her name, according to Merrill Unger, means "'whose father is joy,' no doubt giving a clue to her sunny, joyous, and gracious personality. Just the opposite of her husband, she was generous, kind, and lovely."[2] Most likely joined with Nabal through an arranged marriage, Abigail managed to retain her dignity in spite of her surly husband.

### David

Day in and day out, David's fugitive company has been a shield around Nabal's shepherds and flocks without taking so much as one stray lamb as recompense for their trouble. They've risked their lives for Nabal, and now it's payday.

## A Story of Conflicts

A stubborn husband. A wise wife. A frustrated hero. These players are poised for conflict.

### Between Husband and Wife

Nabal and Abigail differ vastly in temperament, attitude, and philosophy of life. Any woman who lives with a demanding, brutish husband can empathize with Abigail's anguish. As the story progresses, let's see how she manages to remain true to her husband, her Lord, and herself.

### Between Employer and Employee

The main conflict occurs between Nabal and David, who has

---

2. Merrill F. Unger, *Unger's Commentary on the Old Testament* (Chicago, Ill.: Moody Press, 1981), vol. 1, p. 400.

sent some of his men to request their share of the profit. He isn't pushy or grasping in his message; in fact, he is extremely gracious.

> "Go up to Carmel, visit Nabal and greet him in my name; and thus you shall say, 'Have a long life, peace be to you, and peace be to your house, and peace be to all that you have. And now I have heard that you have shearers; now your shepherds have been with us and we have not insulted them, nor have they missed anything all the days they were in Carmel. Ask your young men and they will tell you. Therefore let my young men find favor in your eyes, for we have come on a festive day. Please give whatever you find at hand to your servants and to your son David.'" (1 Sam. 25:5b–8)

But, sneering, Nabal replies:

> "Who is David? And who is the son of Jesse? There are many servants today who are each breaking away from his master. Shall I then take my bread and my water and my meat that I have slaughtered for my shearers, and give it to men whose origin I do not know?" (vv. 10b–11)

Unlike Ahimelech, who was so generous with the ceremonial bread (see 21:1–6), Nabal won't share a single crumb from his table. He snubs the Lord's anointed, calling him a rebellious runaway, and sends the men home empty-handed.

### Between David's Conscience and His Anger

When he hears Nabal's response, David—the paragon of patience and faith—tells his men, "Each of you gird on his sword" (25:13)!

Can this be the same man of God who refused to retaliate against Saul? It sure can. It just goes to show that past victories don't guarantee future successes. Each opportunity for anger carries the same destructive potential. In David's case, it was like a match had been tossed onto a pile of dry hay. In a moment, he was aflame with revenge.

## Conflict Development

While the angry hooves of David's horses thunder in the distance, an unnamed servant warns Abigail of the approaching storm.

### Abigail Is Informed

But one of the young men told Abigail, Nabal's wife, saying, "Behold, David sent messengers from the wilderness to greet our master, and he scorned them. Yet the men were very good to us, and we were not insulted, nor did we miss anything as long as we went about with them, while we were in the fields. They were a wall to us both by night and by day, all the time we were with them tending the sheep. Now therefore, know and consider what you should do, for evil is plotted against our master and against all his household; and he is such a worthless man that no one can speak to him." (vv. 14–17)

Abigail doesn't try to defend Nabal; she knows he's a fool. But she also doesn't give him up to his "fate." Instead, she wisely considers the painful consequences of David's rash act not only for her household and "worthless" husband but especially for David, whose reputation as the soon-to-be king needs protecting. So, without Nabal knowing it, she puts a plan into action.

### Abigail Responds Wisely

Quickly, Abigail gathers a generous amount of food and wine— probably already prepared for Nabal's sheepshearing banquet—and rides off to intercept David in the hills (vv. 18–20). Her intercession is tactful, acknowledging Nabal's fault and respectfully addressing David as "my lord" (vv. 23–25). She also displays her faith, crediting the Lord with both restraining David from murder and forming a new dynasty through him (vv. 26–28). In fact, this "enduring house," David's divine destiny, is something she feels especially protective of.

"And it shall come about when the Lord shall do for my lord according to all the good that He has spoken concerning you, and shall appoint you ruler over Israel, that this will not cause grief or a troubled heart to my lord, both by having shed blood without cause and by my lord having avenged himself. When the Lord shall deal well with my lord, then remember your maidservant." (vv. 30–31)

In all this, however, she remains loyal to Nabal. Although she's honest about his good-for-nothing character, she doesn't join David's band or set up her husband for a fall. Tact, faith, and loyalty—three qualities of a peacemaker. Having had her say, she quietly waits for David's response.

## Supernatural Solutions

As the events play out, all three conflicts are untangled—in reverse order. First, David quiets his anger. Then the hostility between David and Nabal is put to rest. Finally, in a surprising end, the conflict between Abigail and Nabal is resolved.

### Two Conflicts Resolved through Wisdom

Immediately, David embraces Abigail's wise and true words, dismissing the hotheaded vow he'd made earlier (vv. 21–22). He, too, recognizes God's gracious, restraining hand.

> Then David said to Abigail, "Blessed be the Lord God of Israel, who sent you this day to meet me, and blessed be your discernment, and blessed be you, who have kept me this day from bloodshed, and from avenging myself by my own hand. Nevertheless, as the Lord God of Israel lives, who has restrained me from harming you, unless you had come quickly to meet me, surely there would not have been left to Nabal until the morning light as much as one male." So David received from her hand what she had brought him, and he said to her, "Go up to your house in peace. See, I have listened to you and granted your request." (vv. 32–35)

At peace with himself and with Nabal, David bestows peace on the peacemaker. And she turns for home . . . and Nabal.

### One Conflict Resolved through Waiting

Tired and emotionally spent, Abigail walks in the front door and finds Nabal drunk. Wisely, she lets him sleep it off before telling him what happened with David (v. 36). However,

> it came about in the morning, when the wine had gone out of Nabal, that his wife told him these things, and his heart died within him so that he became as a stone. And about ten days later, it happened that

the Lord struck Nabal, and he died. (vv. 37–38)

Suddenly and ironically, the one who had a heart of stone, "became as a stone" and died.

But there's more.

> When David heard that Nabal was dead, he said, "Blessed be the Lord, who has pleaded the cause of my reproach from the hand of Nabal, and has kept back His servant from evil. The Lord has also returned the evildoing of Nabal on his own head." Then David sent a proposal to Abigail, to take her as his wife. (v. 39)

Abigail humbly accepts David's marriage proposal (v. 42). And we see a happy ending for those who placed their trust in God.

## Lessons Learned

It's reassuring to know that yesterday's victories don't have to become today's defeats. By listening to those who can show us all sides of the picture and by being humble enough to admit we're wrong, we can rein in our anger like David did. In short, *When conflicts arise, be wise.* Take time to think and pray; and remember God's care for you and call on your life (see 1 Thess. 2:12).

Abigail teaches us another lesson: *Whenever you realize there's nothing you can do, wait for God's power.* Your story may not resolve as suddenly and dramatically as Abigail's, but what does remain consistent in all human stories is God. When circumstances appear impossible, don't give up hope. Don't keep going in your own strength. Instead, wait . . . and rest . . . on Him.

### A Psalm of David

*I waited patiently for the Lord;*
*And He inclined to me, and heard my cry.*
*He brought me up out of the pit of destruction,*
*    out of the miry clay;*
*And He set my feet upon a rock making my footsteps*
*    firm.*
*And He put a new song in my mouth, a song of*
*    praise to our God;*
*Many will see and fear,*
*And will trust in the Lord.* (Ps. 40:1–3)

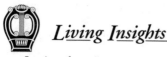 *Living Insights*

Let's play "worst-case scenario." What if David *had* taken revenge?

- What would David have been guilty of (1 Sam. 25:26, 31)?

  _____

- What prerogative would he have taken from God (vv. 26, 31)?

  _____

- What would he have sacrificed (vv. 28, 30)?

  _____

- What would he have gained (v. 31)?

  _____

All because of an impassioned moment of hotheaded revenge.
Suffering an offense from a family member, friend, boss, or coworker—including fellow Christians—naturally pricks our retaliation instincts. But before you know it, a small flame of revenge can grow into an all-consuming blaze, burning yourself and others. What worst-case scenario may result if you try to "even the score" with someone you are in conflict with?

_____

_____

_____

Would that honor God, the other person, or yourself?
David wisely followed Abigail's God-centered advice. The apostles also give us godly advice. Read through the following passages, and select one or two to remember during times of conflict.

## Our Calling and Purpose in God

Romans 12:1–2
1 Thessalonians 2:12

## Specific Guidelines

| | |
|---|---|
| Romans 12:14, 17 | Ephesians 4:29 |
| Romans 12:18 | Ephesians 4:31–32 |
| Romans 12:19–20 | Colossians 3:8–9 |
| Romans 12:21 | Colossians 3:12–17 |
| Galatians 5:13–15 | James 1:19–20 |
| Ephesians 4:1–3 | 1 Peter 3:8–11 |
| Ephesians 4:25–27 | 1 John 4:20–21 |

And remember, you're not on your own. God's Spirit is here to help you, strengthen you, guide you. "Faithful is He who calls you, and He also will bring it to pass" (1 Thess. 5:24; see also Phil. 1:6).

 *Questions for Group Discussion*

1. After showing restraint toward Saul, why do you think David lost control with Nabal?

2. Battling anger is sometimes like bailing water in a storm; just when you toss one bucket of water, another swell washes over the side. Have you ever been surprised by a wave of your own anger? What caused it?

3. What was it about Nabal's response that set David off? What types of people or responses infuriate you?

4. What did Abigail say that opened David's eyes and cooled his rage (see 1 Sam. 25:24–31)?

5. Have you ever tried to reason with an angry person? What lessons do you learn from Abigail's approach?

6. Although he lost his temper at first, David eventually mastered his anger rather than let his anger master him. What's one principle from this story that will help you control your temper?

## Chapter 10

# CLOUDY DAYS ...
# DARK NIGHTS

*1 Samuel 27:1–30:6*

D espite David's vindication over Nabal, life wasn't all tranquillity and joy. Saul's vendetta always lurked in the shadows, even though he had an apparent change of heart at Engedi. The king's pendulum mood might swing at any moment, and the chase might resume with even greater fury.

That dreaded moment came when the Ziphites betrayed David's position, and Saul again called out three thousand troops for a manhunt. David had another tempting opportunity to kill Saul when he crept into the king's camp at night while everyone was asleep. Instead of pinning him to the ground, though, he took Saul's spear and water jug as proof of his mercy. When Saul realized a second time how close he had come to death, he repented and broke off the chase (1 Sam. 26).

Once again, God defied all human odds and delivered the vastly outnumbered David. Yet, instead of firming David's faith, this latest episode left him exhausted. As F. B. Meyer observed, David was nearing the limits of his endurance:

> It had become so increasingly difficult to elude the hot pursuit of the royal troops, whom long practice had familiarized with his hiding-places and haunts. And it became more and more perplexing to find sustenance for the large body of followers now attached to him. Every day he had to provide for six hundred men, besides women and children; and the presence of these more tender souls made it perilously difficult to maintain a perpetual condition of migration or flight.[1]

Unending demands. Constant tension. Increasing danger. How long was God going to keep David on the run? We can understand

---

1. F. B. Meyer, *David: Shepherd, Psalmist, King* (reprint, Fort Washington, Pa.: Christian Literature Crusade, 1977), p. 134.

how he might have slipped into a pit of despair, crying wearily to God,

> How long, O Lord? Wilt Thou forget me forever?
> How long wilt Thou hide Thy face from me?
> How long shall I take counsel in my soul,
> Having sorrow in my heart all the day?
> How long will my enemy be exalted over me?
> (Ps. 13:1–2)

## Clouds and Darkness Come

There is nothing ethically, morally, or spiritually wrong with those feelings of despair that chill us like an unexpected downpour. It's when we take matters into our own hands and flee to a cover of our own choosing that disobedience begins. That's what David did in 1 Samuel 27.

### The Causes

Attempting to solve his problems by his own wits, David only complicated them—as we shall see. His self-spun web of trouble began subtly, almost innocently, with a simple thought:

"Then David said to himself . . ." (v. 1a)

At critical junctures in the past, David usually consulted the Lord (see 23:2, 4). It seems out of character for him to look within for direction. Where is the prophet Gad (see 22:5)? Has David forgotten Abiathar's ephod that helped him make a decision before (see 23:9–12)?[2]

Seeing his situation from his own limited, human point of view, David missed God's perspective and lost his confidence. All at once, Saul loomed larger than Goliath and twice as menacing.

"Now I will perish one day by the hand of Saul." (27:1b)

We can understand David's anxiety; if a madman like Saul was breathing down our necks with an army of three thousand soldiers, we'd fear for our lives too. Yet David was focusing more on his dire straits than on his divine Savior. Hadn't God promised to make him the king of Israel?

2. The ephod was the high priest's garment on which he wore a breastpiece that probably held the Urim and Thummim. The Urim and Thummim were possibly stones that were drawn as yes or no answers to questions posed to the Lord (see Exod. 28:28–30).

Had not these promises been confirmed by Samuel, Jonathan, Abigail, and Saul himself? Had not the golden oil designated him as God's anointed? How impossible it was that God should lie or forget his covenant! By immutable pledges his almighty Friend had bound himself, seeking to give his much-tried child strong consolation, if only he would remain within the sheltering walls of the refuge-harbor which these assurances constituted.[3]

Having concluded that his life was over in Judah, David arrived at the only logical course he could find:

> "There is nothing better for me than to escape into the land of the Philistines. Saul then will despair of searching for me anymore in all the territory of Israel, and I will escape from his hand." (v. 1c)

Was there truly *nothing* better for him than to seek refuge with the Philistines? He could remain in Judah, trusting in the One who had been a constant shield around him. At the very least, he could wait on the Lord for direction. How easy it is for us to justify our actions by saying, "But I had no other choice."

And notice the emphasis on "me" and "I." David's eyes were fixed on himself. But was he the only one affected by his decision?

### The Extent

None of us lives only to ourselves, nor dies to ourselves . . . nor sins to ourselves. Carried along in the wake of David's choice were the people most dear to him.

> So David arose and crossed over, he and the six hundred men who were with him, to Achish the son of Maoch, king of Gath. And David lived with Achish at Gath, he and his men, each with his household, even David with his two wives, Ahinoam the Jezreelitess, and Abigail the Carmelitess, Nabal's widow. (vv. 2–3)

Gath was Goliath's hometown, a center of pagan idolatry. Here, among some of God's vilest enemies, David and his followers made

3. Meyer, *David*, pp. 135–36.

their home. Previously, Achish despised David, but now he respected him as the commander of an impressive guerrilla army. He probably thought that any enemy of Saul's was a friend of his. Friendship with Achish, however, came with a price.

### The Consequences

As payment for his protection, Achish expected loyalty in return—a heavy debt that David may not have bargained on. Several consequences of his decision began emerging.

*He experienced a false sense of security.* Initially, David felt relief. Saul called off the search when he found out that David had escaped deep into Philistine territory (v. 4). The plan worked; David was safe. But it wasn't long before the payments to Achish started coming due.

*He adopted the adversary's cause.* David wasn't really free. He simply traded one master for another. The first hint of David's new relationship with Achish appears in his request for a city to call his home:

> Then David said to Achish, "If now I have found favor in your sight, let them give me a place in one of the cities in the country, that I may live there; for why should your servant live in the royal city with you?" (v. 5)

Did you catch it? David, the anointed king of Israel, called himself the "servant" of Achish.

*He began a period of compromise.* Achish gave Ziklag to David (v. 6), a city to the south that had been a part of Judah until taken over by the Philistines (see Josh. 19:1, 5). The sixteen months David lived there would mark one of the darkest periods in his life (v. 7). He would plunge himself and his followers into an unseemly career of violence and deception. Spiritually, this time offers no psalms pouring from David's heart.

## Winds and Storms Increase

By trying to solve his own problems, David had put himself in a very precarious position. On the one hand, he had to keep Achish convinced he was a Philistine; at the same time, he couldn't let the Hebrews think he was a traitor.

### Duplicity

To demonstrate his loyalty to the Hebrews, David and his men raided Judah's enemies in the south, "the Geshurites and the Girzites and the Amalekites" (v. 8). He took anything of value, "the sheep, the cattle, the donkeys, the camels, and the clothing" (v. 9). The people of Judah were pleased, but what would he say to Achish when it came time to make his report?

### Vagueness

To protect himself, David skirted the truth. He told the king that he was raiding in the Negev (south country) of Judah, which led Achish to believe that he was actually fighting his own people!

### Secrecy

To protect his lies, David became ruthless in his raids.

> And David did not leave a man or a woman alive, to bring to Gath, saying, "Lest they should tell about us, saying, 'So has David done and so has been his practice all the time he has lived in the country of the Philistines.'" (v. 11)

## Injury and Devastation Occur

Achish was so fooled by David's deceit (v. 12) that he wanted to make David his personal bodyguard (28:2). Then, to make matters worse, Achish planned a major assault on Israel—with David and his men right beside him (28:1; 29:1–2)!

See what trouble David caused himself by making a decision out of fear instead of faith? How could he fight against his own people? Yet, if he didn't, his cover would be blown with Achish. What was he to do?

Fortunately, the Philistine military leaders resolved the situation for him. But the solution took its toll.

First, *David became displaced.* Although Achish was fooled by David, the Philistine commanders had their doubts about him. So, before the battle, he was dismissed from his post and sent home. Now he was neither Israelite nor Philistine, a man without an identity (29:3–7).

Second, *he became disillusioned.* David had put his stock in Achish's protection, and now the deal fell through. He thought he had the perfect setup, but his plan backfired. And he had no Plan B to guarantee his safety (vv. 8–11).

Third, *he became depressed.* As he and his men trudged home to Ziklag, they found their territory ash-gray and smoking, their families captured by Amalekites. "Then David and the people who were with him lifted their voices and wept until there was no strength in them to weep" (30:4).

Fourth, *he became distrusted.* So embittered were his men, so angry for having trusted David and lost everything, they started talking about stoning him. At this point, David had sunk to his lowest low (v. 6a). Finally, he was ready to reach out to heaven.

## Timeless Truth

Meyer vividly pictures this moment of truth in David's life:

> In that dread hour, with the charred embers smoking at his feet; with the cold hand of anxiety for the fate of his wives feeling at his heart; with the sense of duplicity and deceit which he had been practising, and which had alienated him from God, on his conscience; with this threat of stoning in his ears, his heart suddenly sprang back into its old resting-place in the bosom of God.[4]

The biblical historian writes simply, "David strengthened himself in the Lord his God" (v. 6b). Out of the miry pit of his own making, David stepped into the refreshing pool of God's mercy and cleansed himself of all pride. Then he did what he should have done in the first place. He called to Abiathar the priest, "Please bring me the ephod" (v. 7). He was determined to look to the Lord for guidance in his next decision regarding whether to pursue the Amalekites. He'd learned his lesson. No more stepping ahead of the Lord.

Where do you look for guidance and strength when you're nearing the limits of your endurance? The principle we learn from David's experience is this: *cloudy days and dark nights call for right thinking and a vertical focus.* Our feet may slip in the mire of despair; our friends may scatter like dry leaves; but help is never far away, as long as we keep looking up.

4. Meyer, *David*, pp. 147–48.

## A Psalm of David

*O Lord my God,*
*I cried to Thee for help, and Thou didst heal me.*
*O Lord, Thou hast brought up my soul from Sheol;*
*Thou hast kept me alive, that I should not go down to*
*    the pit.*
*Sing praise to the Lord, you His godly ones,*
*And give thanks to His holy name.*
*For His anger is but for a moment,*
*His favor is for a lifetime;*
*Weeping may last for the night,*
*But a shout of joy comes in the morning.* (Ps. 30:2–5)

 *Living Insights*

The wind is a force without a conscience, completely unpredictable and out of control. One day, it plays softly among the trees. The next day, it roars angrily, snapping giant elms like twigs. It swells over the mountains and shrieks through the canyons, howling like a mythical beast unleashed from the netherworld. The sturdiest buildings tremble against its raging. Loose cables slap and whip; shutters bang, bang-bang in a rhythmless cadence.

Then it stops. Its fury is exhausted . . . but for how long?

To David, King Saul must have seemed like the wind, but even more erratic and violent. What was it like to live at the mercy of a madman? Put yourself in David's worn-out sandals. What doubts and fears may have been coursing through his heart (see 1 Sam. 27:1)?

_____

_____

_____

Has a howling wind been shaking your rafters lately, perhaps in the form of a lost job, a turbulent relationship, a financial problem, or a physical hardship? If so, what doubts and fears have you been feeling?

_____

_____

Fear hindered David in two ways: first, it kept him focused on his circumstances rather than on the Lord; and second, it backed him into making a rash decision when he should have waited on the Lord. Has fear affected you in a similar way? Have you made any decisions that you now regret?

_____

_____

_____

As David discovered, it's never too late to strengthen yourself in the Lord. Take a few moments to pray through David's moving words of faith in Psalm 31:1–5. Against the furious and unpredictable winds of life, there is no safer place to find shelter than within the refuge of God's strength.

 *Questions for Group Discussion*

1. At the beginning of today's passage, Saul is after David, but by the end, his own men are at his throat. Talk about going from bad to worse. Let's look at David's downward spiral one step at a time. What do you think was his first mistake (see 27:1)?

2. When we feed our fears like David did, they grow until they consume our faith in God. What are some ways we can we keep our fears under control?

3. Fleeing to Philistia was like running into a lion's den to escape a bear. What are some unwise places we run to to escape our fears and troubles?

4. David's lies worked well—too well. David had Achish so convinced that he was loyal to the Philistines that Achish enlisted him in the fight against Israel. For David to fight with the Philistines against Saul would have jeopardized his chances of becoming king. How did God save David from his own foolish mistakes (see 1 Sam. 29:3–11)? Why do you think God intervened?

5. What was God teaching David through the Ziklag experience (see 30:1–8)?

6. What lesson is God teaching you through David's example?

Chapter 11

# TWO DEATHS . . .
# A STUDY IN CONTRAST

*1 Samuel 31*

As David surveyed the smoking rubble that was once Ziklag, he saw through tear-filled eyes the results of his own faulty leadership. His flight to Philistia was meant to provide safety and shelter for his people. His intentions were good, but he was leading in the flesh, out of fear and panic. He had charted a course apart from the Lord and brought disaster on his followers.

If David was going to be king of Israel, he needed to put to death any part of himself that acted independently of God. He must rule the nation according to God's will, not his.

Tragically, Saul never learned that lesson. While David repented in the ashes of Ziklag and strengthened himself in the Lord, Saul stood in his own strength against the Philistines at Jezreel.

While David consulted the Lord through the ephod of Abiathar the priest, Saul consulted a spiritist at En-dor (see 1 Sam. 28).

And while David pursued the Amalekites, rescuing his family and restoring his faith, Saul went down in defeat to the Philistines, losing his family, his kingdom, and his life.

## Saul's Demise: Pathetic Tragedy

Few have had beginnings as bright as Saul's. Physically, he stood head and shoulders above all the people (1 Sam. 9:2). In his character, initially, he was modest and unpretentious (v. 21). Spiritually, he was anointed by God and divinely equipped with the heart and the power to lead the nation according to God's ways (10:1–13). He had it all. Yet from that high and noble beginning, Saul sank to an infamous ending.

In a vulnerable moment before David, he uttered what has come to be his epitaph,

"Behold, I have played the fool." (26:21b)

Commentator J. Sidlow Baxter points out the essential sin that led to Saul's foolishness—self-will.

Let us mark this well—Saul was called to *theocratic* kingship. . . . Saul was never meant to have a kingship of *absolute* power. It was never intended that the last word should be with *him*. He was anointed of God to be the executor of a will higher than his own. He was to be the human and visible vice-regent of Israel's Divine and invisible King, Jehovah. He could only truly rule the subjects beneath him to the extent in which he obeyed the supreme King above him.

. . . The Philistines were not Saul's worst enemies. His worst foe was himself. Every man who lets "self" fill his vision till it blinds his inner eye to what is really true and Divine is "playing the fool."[1]

Saul's downhill slide did not happen overnight but over many years. And ultimately, like a rotting tree collapsing on itself, his self-centeredness and self-will ended in self-destruction.

### The Battle: A Slaughter

Scripture never pales the truth. In 1 Samuel 31, we read about an ugly battle between Israel and Philistia—the battle that would be Saul's last.

Now the Philistines were fighting against Israel, and the men of Israel fled from before the Philistines and fell slain on Mount Gilboa. And the Philistines overtook Saul and his sons; and the Philistines killed Jonathan and Abinadab and Malchi-shua the sons of Saul. And the battle went heavily against Saul, and the archers hit him; and he was badly wounded by the archers. Then Saul said to his armor bearer, "Draw your sword and pierce me through with it, lest these uncircumcised come and pierce me through and make sport of me." (vv. 1–4a)

Saul figured it was better to die quickly at the hand of a trusted friend than in slow agony at the hand of a sadistic enemy. Perhaps the saddest part of this scene is what Saul didn't say. Even in his

---

1. J. Sidlow Baxter, *Explore the Book*, 6 vols. in 1 (Grand Rapids, Mich.: Zondervan Publishing House, Academie Books, 1966), vol. 2, p. 60.

final moments, he neglected to call out to God. No repentance. No reconciliation. Saul faced death as he faced life: with his eyes desperately fixed on his circumstances and himself.

### The Death: A Suicide

Afraid of killing the Lord's anointed, his armor bearer refused his master's request (compare 2 Sam. 1:14).

> So Saul took his sword and fell on it. And when his armor bearer saw that Saul was dead, he also fell on his sword and died with him.[2] Thus Saul died with his three sons, his armor bearer, and all his men on that day together. (1 Sam. 31:4b–6)

Saul's sins cost him his life—but not his only. How many innocent people, including godly Jonathan, suffered and died that day because of the consequences of Saul's sin? We must never think that we live or die only to ourselves.

## The Philistines' Response: Sadistic Brutality

Having broken Israel's defenses, the Philistine army drove like a lance through the heart of Israel all the way to the Transjordan.

> And when the men of Israel who were on the other side of the valley, with those who were beyond the Jordan, saw that the men of Israel had fled and that Saul and his sons were dead, they abandoned the cities and fled; then the Philistines came and lived in them. (v. 7)

The Philistines had successfully divided Israel and taken command of several strategic inland trade centers. For the Philistines, who had been confined to the coastal plains since the period of the Judges, it was a sweet victory. Not only did it promise to increase their wealth and power, but in their thinking, it demonstrated the supremacy of their gods. They determined to exploit this triumph to the fullest.

---

2. The Bible records three other people who took their own lives: Ahithophel (2 Sam. 17:23), Zimri (1 Kings 16:18), and Judas (Matt. 27:5). Each case is a tragic expression of despair. Scripture never condones or glorifies suicide.

## Exploitation

> And it came about on the next day when the Phi-
> listines came to strip the slain, that they found Saul
> and his three sons fallen on Mount Gilboa. And
> they cut off his head, and stripped off his weapons,
> and sent them throughout the land of the Philis-
> tines, to carry the good news to the house of their
> idols and to the people. And they put his weapons
> in the temple of Ashtaroth, and they fastened his
> body to the wall of Beth-shan. (vv. 8–10)

On the wall of the great fortress Beth-shan, the Philistines hung
their ghastly trophies: the mutilated bodies of Saul and, as verse 12
tells us, his three sons.

## Cremation

Word of the travesty traveled across the Jordan river to Jabesh-
gilead, the Israelite settlement that Saul had rescued from the Ammonites early in his career (see 1 Sam. 11). That magnificent victory forty years before had won the heart of the nation and roused
the people to acclaim Saul their king. "That had been the morning
of Saul's life, bright and promising as none other," writes Bible
historian Alfred Edersheim,

> and now it was night; and the headless bodies of
> Saul and his sons, deserted by all, swung in the wind
> on the walls of Bethshan, amid the hoarse music of
> vultures and jackals.[3]

How far Saul had fallen! And the tragedy of it all was this: it
need never have been. Had Saul bent his will to God's will and
rested in Him, had he obeyed God and loved Him with his whole
heart, Saul could have been Israel's greatest king (see 13:13–14).

As it was, he died in shame. In an ironic twist, his story comes
full circle as the men of Jabesh-gilead "rescue" him.

> When the inhabitants of Jabesh-gilead heard what
> the Philistines had done to Saul, all the valiant men
> rose and walked all night, and took the body of Saul

---

3. Alfred Edersheim, *Bible History: Old Testament,* 7 vols. in 1 (1982; reprint, Grand Rapids,
Mich.: William B. Eerdmans Publishing Co., 1987), vol. 4, p. 149.

and the bodies of his sons from the wall of Beth-shan, and they came to Jabesh, and burned them there.[4] And they took their bones and buried them under the tamarisk tree at Jabesh, and fasted seven days. (vv. 11–13)

With these stark and mournful words, the book of 1 Samuel ends and the curtain closes on the life of Israel's first and most tragic king.

## Christ's Death: Classic Analogy

Saul's death was an ending—full of sorrow and regret—but it was also a beginning. In 2 Samuel, the curtain will rise again, eventually revealing a new and hopeful day as Israel awakens to her wise shepherd-king, David.

In this way, perhaps, Saul's death serves as an analogy to Christ's crucifixion. Saul's death appeared to signal the end of all hope in Israel; Christ's death, the end of all spiritual hope. When Saul died, it seemed as though the enemy had finally defeated Israel; when Christ died, it seemed as though Satan had won. Saul's death paved the way for a new and better regime; and Christ's death paved the way for an entirely new plan of grace, opening the door to all who would come to God in faith.

### A Psalm of David

*Then David chanted with this lament over Saul and*
*Jonathan his son, . . .*
*"Your beauty, O Israel, is slain on your high places!*
*How have the mighty fallen!*
*Tell it not in Gath,*
*Proclaim it not in the streets of Ashkelon;*
*Lest the daughters of the Philistines rejoice,*
*Lest the daughters of the uncircumcised exult.*
*O mountains of Gilboa,*
*Let not dew or rain be on you, nor fields of offerings;*
*For there the shield of the mighty was defiled,*
*The shield of Saul, not anointed with oil.*

---

4. Since the Bible is silent on the issue of cremation, individual preferences in taking care of a loved one's remains should be respected. Certainly, cremation will not hinder God from giving a person a glorified body on the day of resurrection (see 1 Cor. 15:50–54; 2 Cor. 5:1–5; 1 John 3:2).

*From the blood of the slain, from the fat of the mighty,*
*The bow of Jonathan did not turn back,*
*And the sword of Saul did not return empty.*
*Saul and Jonathan, beloved and pleasant in their life,*
*And in their death they were not parted;*
*They were swifter than eagles,*
*They were stronger than lions.*
*O daughters of Israel, weep over Saul,*
*Who clothed you luxuriously in scarlet,*
*Who put ornaments of gold on your apparel.*
*How have the mighty fallen in the midst of the battle!*
*Jonathan is slain on your high places.*
*I am distressed for you, my brother Jonathan;*
*You have been very pleasant to me.*
*Your love to me was more wonderful*
*Than the love of women.*
*How have the mighty fallen,*
*And the weapons of war perished!"*
*(2 Sam. 1:17, 19–27)*

 ## *Living Insights*

J. Sidlow Baxter draws from Saul's life a sober warning about ruling our lives independently of God:

> [Saul] could only truly rule the subjects beneath him to the extent in which he obeyed the supreme King above him. So is it with ourselves. We are not the independent proprietors of our own beings. We are God's property. He has made us kings and queens over our own personalities with their gifts and powers and possibilities; but our rule is meant to be theocratic, not an independent, self-directed monarchy. We are meant to rule for God, so that our lives and personalities may fulfill His will and accomplish His purpose. When we obstinately rule independently of God our true kingship breaks down; we lose the true meaning and purpose of life. In greater or lesser degree we "play the fool."[5]

5. Baxter, *Explore the Book*, vol. 2, p. 60.

How have you been ruling your life? As "an independent, self-directed monarchy"? Or as a theocracy with God as the head?

_____

_____

_____

Can you see any ways that you might be "playing the fool," perhaps by stepping ahead of God or by partially obeying His will?

_____

_____

_____

If Saul's life teaches us anything, it's that opportunity does not necessarily make a good king. Endowments alone, either physical or spiritual, are no guarantee of success. As you close this chapter, ask yourself prayerfully, "What advantages has God given me? And what can I do to keep my life on God's course?"

## Questions for Group Discussion

1. Saul made a shambles of his life. In your opinion, where did he go wrong? (For examples, see 1 Sam. 13:8–14; 15; 23:19–24; 26:1–6.)

2. We normally think of Saul and David at opposite ends of a pole. Consider, however, how Saul and David began their careers. In what ways were they similar?

3. Picture David standing among the smoldering consequences of his sin at Ziklag and then, a few days later, hearing about Saul's tragic death. How do you think the two events side-by-side may have impacted him? What sober warning was God giving him?

4. Saul's anointing didn't immunize him from failure, and neither would David's. As you reflect on Psalm 103:15–22, what does David tell us is vital to lasting success?

5. In what ways can you use these insights in your life this week?

## 🔨 Digging Deeper

Suicide. For some of you, the word has the academic feel of a classroom discussion. For others, it hits all too close to home. Maybe someone you loved saw it as a solution, or maybe thoughts of suicide creep into your mind when life's pain seems too much to bear.

God has instilled in each of us a strong instinct to live. But sometimes, when a deep sense of failure or loneliness or despair sets in, this desire to live is quelled by an even stronger desire to die.

Fortunately, potential suicide victims usually communicate their pain before acting, making suicide preventable if those near know the signals.

We've supplied you with a list of these warning signs to help alert you to the suicidal person's subtle cries for help.

- Talking about suicide

- An obsession with death or heaven

- A sudden change in personality

- Deep depression, with symptoms ranging from severe despondency to loss of enjoyment in daily activities

- Physical symptoms: sleeplessness, loss of appetite, decreased sex drive, drastic weight loss, chronic exhaustion

- Crisis situations: death of a loved one, failure at school, loss of a job, marital or home problems, a chronic or terminal illness

- Unprompted preparations for death that may include giving away prized possessions or discussing last wishes with friends and family.

If you recognize any of these signals in yourself or in someone you love, we urge you to get help from the following resources.

### Scripture

Scripture teaches three truths that encourage us to value our lives. First, life is a gift from God to be cherished (Gen. 2:7; John 1:3). Second, the One who gives life is the only one with authority to take it (1 Sam. 2:6; Ps. 31:15a). And third, Scripture prohibits murder, which would include taking your own life (Exod. 20:13).

### Books

Anderson, S. J. *When Someone Wants to Die*. Downers Grove, Ill.: InterVarsity Press, 1988.

Hart, Archibald, D. *Counseling the Depressed*. Resources for Christian Counseling series. Vol. 5. Ed. Gary R. Collins. Dallas, Tex.: Word Publishing, 1987.

Powell, Donalyn. *A Reason to Live*. Minneapolis, Minn.: Bethany House Publishers, 1989.

Wright, H. Norman. *Crisis Counseling: What to Do and Say During the First 72 Hours*. Ventura, Calif.: Gospel Light Publications, Regal Books, 1993.

### Suicide Prevention and Intervention Organizations

- The American Association of Suicidology, 4201 Connecticut Ave., NW, Suite 408, Washington, DC 20008. (202) 237-2280; Website: www.suicidology.org. Educational information is available, as well as guidelines for starting crisis facilities.

- National Institute of Mental Health (NIMH), Public Inquiries, 6001 Executive Blvd., Rm. 8184 MSC 9663 Bethesda, MD 20892-9663 U.S.A.; e-mail: nimhinfo@nih.gov; www.nimh.nih.gov (301) 443-4513. Information on suicide and related subjects is available.

### Crisis Intervention Hotlines

If you feel like you've reached a point of desperation in your life, please realize that there is help from people who care. Many crisis intervention agencies are open twenty-four hours a day and can provide you with counseling and referrals. To get in touch with one of these agencies, please consult your local telephone book under Crisis Intervention or call the National Hopeline Network hotline at 1-800-SUICIDE.

## Chapter 12

# NEW KING, NEW THRONE, SAME LORD

*Selected Scriptures*

So far, we've traced the events of David's life from his humble beginnings as a shepherd boy to his glory days as a national hero, from his pinnacle of success as a valiant commander in Saul's army to his pit of despair as an outlaw in the wilderness. Now, with Saul's death, David's story takes a long-awaited turn: finally the outlaw is about to become king.

This is a critical juncture in David's life. It's as if he stands on a mountain peak, with all the events of his past behind him like a distant mountain range and all the events of his future spread before him like a vast green valley. It certainly warrants our taking a moment to pause at this strategic lookout and survey what has come before and what lies ahead.

## Panoramic View of David's Life

Peering through the lens of Psalm 78:70–72, we discover a distillation of David's life.

> He also chose David His servant,
> And took him from the sheepfolds;
> From the care of the ewes with suckling lambs He
> brought him,
> To shepherd Jacob His people,
> And Israel His inheritance.
> So he shepherded them according to the integrity
> of his heart,
> And guided them with his skillful hands.

The psalmist's pen sweeps across the years, revealing God's hand in bringing David from leading sheep to shepherding the nation. In each phase of David's life, God has been an ever-present influence—guiding his stone to its mark on Goliath's skull, frustrating Saul's murderous attacks, directing David's movements in the wilderness. In response to God's sovereign grace, David leads the people with integrity and skill.

Does that mean that David never sinned or erred in judgment? Certainly not. Indiscretion and failure shaped his life just as much as virtue and victory. In fact, a diagram of David's life resembles the up-and-down form of a rooftop, with triumph typifying the first part and trouble, the second part.

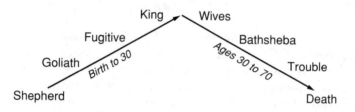

Unlike Michelangelo's marble image of David, the real David had feet of clay. As we focus on his years as king, we'll get a closer look at what made him both an icon of integrity—a man after God's heart—and a man of flesh and blood who, like all of us, was prone to fall.

## Focusing on David's Life as King

Second Samuel 5:4–5 surveys David's reign:

> David was thirty years old when he became king, and he reigned forty years. At Hebron he reigned over Judah seven years and six months, and in Jerusalem he reigned thirty-three years over all Israel and Judah.

David's forty-year career as king was divided into two stages, first as king of the southern tribe of Judah, then as king of all the tribes in the north and the south.

### King over Judah in Hebron

When David heard of Saul's fate, he didn't clap his hands and greedily plot his next move. In genuine grief, he mourned over the death of Saul as well as his beloved friend Jonathan (1:17–27). Then, with a patient and sensitive spirit, he turned to the Lord for guidance: "Shall I go up to one of the cities of Judah?" (2:1).

God directed him to Hebron, where the people of Judah anointed him as their king (vv. 1–7). In time, another of Saul's sons, Ish-bosheth, became the king of the northern tribes, collectively known as "Israel" (see 2 Sam. 2:8–11).[1] During this period, an ugly rift formed between the north and south that would appear again generations later. Tribe fought against tribe, Hebrew against Hebrew, as the house of David and the house of Saul battled for supremacy. And "David grew steadily stronger, but the house of Saul grew weaker continually" (3:1).

During his seven and a half years in Hebron, David continued his practice of polygamy, which, although common among monarchs of the day, was forbidden by God (see Deut. 17:17). Besides Michal (who later became his wife again), David already had two wives—Ahinoam and Abigail. But they weren't enough for him. He married four more women. Then, after he moved to Jerusalem, he added Bathsheba to his harem as well as many other wives and concubines not named in Scripture (5:13). Needless to say, as these women bore children, David's family grew very large.

| DAVID'S IMMEDIATE FAMILY | |
| --- | --- |
| **Children Born in Hebron—David, Age 30–37** (2 Sam. 3:2–5, 13–14; 13:1; 1 Chron. 3:1–4) | |
| *Wives* | *Children* |
| Ahinoam | → Amnon |
| Abigail | → Chileab (Daniel) |
| Maacah | → Absalom and Tamar |
| Haggith | → Adonijah |
| Abital | → Shephatiah |
| Eglah | → Ithream |
| Michal (barren) | |
| **Children Born in Jerusalem—David, Age 37–70** (2 Sam. 5:14–16; 12:25; 1 Chron. 3:5–8; 14:4–7; 2 Chron. 11:18) | |
| *Wives* | *Children* |
| Bathsheba (Bath-shua) | → Shammua (Shimea), Shobab, Nathan, Solomon (Jedediah) |
| Unnamed Wives | → Ibhar, Elishua (Elishama), Eliphelet (Elpelet), Nogah, Nepheg, Japhia, Elishama, Eliada (Beeliada), Eliphelet, Jerimoth |

The total size of David's immediate family is twenty sons and one daughter (1 Chron. 3:9). This excludes concubines and their offspring, which are not named in Scripture; see 2 Sam. 5:13; 15:16; 1 Chron. 3:9.[2]

1. Ish-bosheth reigned only two years (2 Sam. 2:10), which probably constituted the final two years of David's seven-and-a-half-year reign of Judah because David assumed control of Israel immediately after Ish-bosheth's death (2 Sam. 4:1–5:3). During the first five and a half years after Saul's death, Israel apparently had no king, or perhaps Abner, Saul's general, ruled the country.

2. Adapted from Charles R. Swindoll, *David: A Man of Passion and Destiny* (Dallas, Tex.: Word Publishing, 1997), p. 134.

### King over All Israel in Jerusalem

Although Ish-bosheth wore the crown in Israel, the general of Israel's army, Abner, held the power. He was the one who made Ish-bosheth king (2 Sam. 2:8–9). So when Joab (David's army general) killed Abner, Ish-bosheth "lost courage, and all Israel was disturbed" (4:1). It was only a matter of time before David's forces would conquer the weakened house of Israel.

That final battle never happened, though, because Ish-bosheth was assassinated by two of his own captains. With a flash of their sword, Saul's troubled dynasty ended forever. Soon after, the elders of Israel approached David at Hebron and anointed him as their king. At last, the nation was united again (5:1–3).

David was immediately faced with a serious diplomatic dilemma: Where would he set up his capital? To remain in Judah would alienate Israel; to move north to Israel would insult Judah. In a brilliant political maneuver, David invaded the small Jebusite stronghold located in the middle of the nation, the city of Jebus (see 1 Chron. 11:4). Jebus was neither Israel nor Judah—the perfect neutral ground where both sides could join together as one. David took Jebus and fittingly renamed it Jerusalem, the City of Peace (2 Sam. 5:6–9).

> And David became greater and greater, for the Lord
> God of hosts was with him. (v. 10)

David's many accomplishments as Israel's king sparkled like the jewels in his crown.

- He expanded Israel's boundaries from six thousand to sixty thousand square miles.

- He set up extensive trade routes.

- He unified the nation.

- He subdued Israel's enemies more completely than anyone had done since Joshua's time.

- He shaped a national interest in spiritual concerns.

As impressive as David's achievements were, the disappointments from his reign cast somber shadows across his legacy. First, *he became so enamored with public pursuits that he lost control of his family.* Just because David could rule a nation didn't mean he knew how to run his home. At times, David seemed almost helpless in dealing with his children. When Amnon raped his half sister, Tamar, David got angry—but did nothing (13:21). When Absalom rebelled, David remained aloof (chaps. 14–15). And when Adonijah exalted himself, saying, "I will be king," David never rebuked him or questioned his actions (1 Kings 1:5–6).

Second, *he indulged himself in extravagant activities of passion.* While his army was off fighting the Ammonites, he stayed home and lounged at his palace (2 Sam. 11:1). This inappropriate season of leisure became an opportunity for lust when David spied the alluring (and already married) Bathsheba from his rooftop. David had plenty of wives and even concubines, but he didn't have Bathsheba. The flesh always wants what it doesn't have. So David took Bathsheba for himself, and out of that one moment of passion poured a lifetime of turmoil and pain.

Third, *he became a victim of self-sufficiency and pride.* Near the end of David's life, he took a census of the people to calculate the potential size of his army (24:1–3; 1 Chron. 21:1–7, 14). What's wrong with that? David was glorying in his own strength rather than the Lord's, and as a result, God sent a plague on the people as judgment. Seventy thousand people died because of his sin—a fact that shot like a flaming arrow into his conscience and burned into him a hard lesson about the deadly power of pride.

## Timeless and Priceless Truths to Live By

Our survey of David's life teaches at least two important truths about our family and our character.

*No personal pursuit is more important than cultivating godliness into your family.* David could build a nation but he couldn't build a godly home. Surely, he would have given everything—his power, his wealth, his fame—to have children who feared the Lord. Busy building an empire? What is it costing your family?

*No character trait needs more attention than integrity.* When David relaxed his attention for a moment, a look turned into lust, and a night of passion turned into a nightmare of deception, murder, and regret. That can just as easily happen to us too, so we must be diligent in cultivating such seeds of integrity as honesty, authenticity, standing alone, loyalty to principle, keeping our word, and especially harmony between public and private life.

## A Concluding Thought

David never did anything halfway. Passionate, magnetic, and determined, he climbed to the heights of success as a military and political champion. Yet the same qualities that propelled him to the top in one setting could suddenly send him plummeting to the bottom in another.

So how did this sin-stained person become the "man after God's own heart"? What does that mean? More than anything else, it refers to his undying and ever-surging love for God. Commentator Alexander Whyte once wrote,

> To know God, and to be in constant communion with God, this is life to David; this is better than life; this is love; this is blessedness.[3]

This is what made David—despite his many failings—a man after God's own heart.

### A Psalm of David

*O God, Thou art my God; I shall seek Thee earnestly;*
*My soul thirsts for Thee, my flesh yearns for Thee,*
*In a dry and weary land where there is no water.*
*Thus I have beheld Thee in the sanctuary,*
*To see Thy power and Thy glory.*
*Because Thy lovingkindness is better than life,*
*My lips will praise Thee.*
*So I will bless Thee as long as I live;*
*I will lift up my hands in Thy name.*
*(Ps. 63:1–4)*

## Living Insights

We've come to an important crossroads in David's life and the midpoint of our study. This makes a good stopping place where we can stretch a little, get our bearings, and see how far we've come.

God has taken David from a "nobody, nobody noticed" to king of Israel. What are a few of the ways God has worked behind the scenes to bring David to this point? (For example, think about some

---

3. Alexander Whyte, *Bible Characters* (1952; reprint, Grand Rapids, Mich.: Zondervan Publishing House, 1959), p. 259.

of the people God brought into David's life or the ways He has protected him.)

_____

_____

_____

David has had to travel a rocky road to the throne. Yet all his blistering days and shivering nights in the desert have taught him valuable lessons about his Lord that will sustain him during his years as king. What are a couple of lessons about God you have learned as you traveled with David?

_____

_____

_____

As rough as his early years of adversity were, his later years of prosperity will be even rougher. Having conquered his external foes, middle-aged David will face the Goliaths within—laziness, lust, hypocrisy, pride.

As we prepare to study this stage of David's life, take a few moments to reflect on the different stages in your life. When have you felt closer to the Lord—during times of adversity or prosperity? Why was that so?

_____

_____

As we enter David's middle and later years, what do you hope to learn from his life?

_____

_____

## Questions for Group Discussion

For this chapter, use the questions from the Living Insights section for your group discussion.

# Chapter 13

# DAVID AND THE ARK
### 2 Samuel 6

**A**ll the words ever spoken about David, the accolades given, and the books written can be summed up in one simple yet poignant statement: David loved God.

We may marvel at his leadership abilities. We may delight in his poetic artistry. We may admire his military prowess. But David's love for God was his quintessential attribute, the sun around which all his other qualities revolved.

David's psalms breathe his affection for the Lord. "O God . . . my soul thirsts for you, my body longs for you," he wrote passionately (Ps. 63:1 NIV). "Your love is better than life," he cried out from the depths of his being (v. 3 NIV). Even in the stillness of the night, his yearnings for God swelled within him. "On my bed I remember you; I think of you through the watches of the night. . . . My soul clings to you" (vv. 6, 8 NIV).

Yes, David loved God. And now that he was king of Israel, he was eager to express his devotion to its fullest measure. Worship meant little to Saul, who had no heart for God. David, however, resolved to set the worship of God as the cornerstone of his government—foreshadowing the government of the messianic kingdom.

His first task was to bring the ark of the covenant to Jerusalem. Long ago, it had resided in the tabernacle at Shiloh with Eli the high priest. Since that time, the ark had been captured by the Philistines, returned to Beth-shemesh, and eventually deposited at the house of Abinadab at Kiriath-jearim. There it remained for more than sixty years, untouched and, in many people's minds, forgotten (see 1 Sam. 4–7:3).[1]

In the process of transporting the ark, however, David learned a vital lesson about how to worship a holy and awesome God. As heartfelt as it may be, love alone is not enough. The apostle John

---

1. The fate of the tabernacle is less clear. After the Philistines captured the ark, Samuel probably moved the tabernacle to the safety of Nob, where it remained until Saul murdered Ahimelech and his line of priests (except Abiathar). Saul then moved the tabernacle to Gibeon, placing it in the care of Zadok, also a descendent of Aaron. It remained in Gibeon during David's reign (see 1 Chron. 16:37–40; 2 Chron. 1:3–4) and wasn't moved to Jerusalem until Solomon built the temple.

instructs, "For this is the love of God, that we keep His command-ments" (1 John 5:3a). To really love God is to obey Him—not just in the principles of His Word, but in the detailed and specific precepts as well.

## Transporting the Ark

What was the ark? Why was it essential to Israel's worship? The answers to these questions help us understand the preciousness of the item David was attempting to move.

### The Ark

The ark was a chest made of acacia wood, gold-plated inside and out, and rimmed with a border of gold. It was $3\,^3/_4$ feet long, $2\,^1/_4$ feet wide, and $2\,^1/_4$ feet high. Its pure gold lid—the mercy seat—was the base for two cherubs of hammered gold, with wings outstretched and touching over the cover (see Exod. 25:10–22). The ark held only three objects: a golden jar containing manna, Aaron's rod, and the Ten Commandments (Heb. 9:4).

*The Ark of the Covenant*

More than an ornate box, the ark represented God's covenant with Israel. It was God's point of contact with sinful humanity. Kept behind the veil of the Holy of Holies, it was visited only once per year by the high priest, who sprinkled blood on the mercy seat and atoned for his sins and the sins of the nation (Heb. 9:3–7). God Himself would meet the priest there, appearing in a cloud over the mercy seat (Lev. 16:2–17). The ark was the symbolic embodiment of the power and presence of God.

Because the ark was holy, God didn't want it hauled around like any old piece of furniture. It had to be handled with reverence and fear. Gold rings were fixed at the corners of both long sides of the ark, and gold-plated poles were slipped through the rings so the ark could be carried without being touched (Exod. 25:12–15). Only Levites could transport the ark (Num. 3:5–10; 4:15; Deut. 10:8).

### The Death

In his zeal, however, David neglected to follow God's instructions on how to transport the ark. Eager to bring it to Jerusalem and begin worshiping the Lord, he "gathered all the chosen men of Israel, thirty thousand" (2 Sam. 6:1) and led them to Kiriath-jearim[2]

> to bring up from there the ark of God which is called by the Name, the very name of the Lord of hosts who is enthroned above the cherubim. And they placed the ark of God on a new cart that they might bring it from the house of Abinadab which was on the hill; and Uzzah and Ahio, the sons of Abinadab, were leading the new cart. . . .
>
> But when they came to the threshing floor of Nacon, Uzzah reached out toward the ark of God and took hold of it, for the oxen nearly upset it. (vv. 2–3, 6)

Instead of being carried with poles on the shoulders of Levites, the ark bumped around on a cart. And, though Uzzah had noble intentions, he touched the ark, thus desecrating its holiness. Clearly, David had overlooked the precepts of God's law—an oversight that cost Uzzah his life.

> And the anger of the Lord burned against Uzzah, and God struck him down there for his irreverence; and he died there by the ark of God. (v. 7)

2. Baale-Judah in verse 2 is the same city as Kiriath-jearim.

As Uzzah slumped beside the ark, panic jerked the procession to a halt. The lyres, harps, and cymbals fell silent. The joyous singing turned to gasps of fear. The people shrank back in terror from the ark and Uzzah's dead body.

When David saw what had happened, he

> became angry because of the Lord's outburst against Uzzah, and that place is called Perez-uzzah to this day. So David was afraid of the Lord that day; and he said, "How can the ark of the Lord come to me?" (vv. 8–9)

He couldn't understand what went wrong. Is this how God repays devotion—with death? David's frustration, combined with humiliation and disappointment, erupted into anger—anger at a God who refused to act according to David's plan.

The fact is, God is God. And He cannot be worshipped in a way that violates His holiness. As sinners, we must come to Him on His terms. We must bend our wills to His, not vice versa. Rushing into His presence our way is as dangerous as thrusting our hand into a flame to get warm. God gave the Law and ultimately sent Jesus to provide us a path through His holiness to His presence. That's why obedience is so important. No matter how much we desire to do the right thing, if we do it the wrong way, we deceive ourselves and worse, we dishonor God.

Too distraught and afraid to finish the trip, David dismissed the throngs and stored the ark at the house of Obed-edom the Gittite, where it stayed for three months. The Lord blessed Obed-edom, and the king took time to ponder his mistake (vv. 10–11). David wasn't perfect, but he *was* sensitive to sin. He admitted his wrong and humbly changed his ways. Unlike Saul, he had a deep yearning to do God's will, even the specific details. That's what made him a man after God's heart.

### The Change

> Now it was told King David, saying, "The Lord has blessed the house of Obed-edom and all that belongs to him, on account of the ark of God." And David went and brought up the ark of God from the house of Obed-edom into the city of David with gladness. (v. 12)

What happened to make David try again? A parallel passage, 1 Chronicles 15:11–15, gives us some behind-the-scenes information. Following Uzzah's tragic death, David did his homework and, with the help of the Levites and priests, discovered the proper way to transport the ark. In David's words to the Levites, notice his honest assessment of his sin against God.

> "Because you did not carry it at the first, the Lord our God made an outburst on us, for we did not seek Him according to the ordinance." (v. 13)

David not only admitted his wrong, the next time around he made it right.

> And the sons of the Levites carried the ark of God on their shoulders, with the poles thereon as Moses had commanded according to the word of the Lord. (v. 15)

## Celebrating the Lord

Some might think that following every detail of God's law would make you unbending, stern, and joyless. But this wasn't the case with David. When the ark finally reached Jerusalem, David celebrated in a way that was anything but rigid.

### David's Dance

> And David was dancing before the Lord with all his might, and David was wearing a linen ephod. So David and all the house of Israel were bringing up the ark of the Lord with shouting and the sound of the trumpet. (2 Sam. 6:14–15)

W. Phillip Keller comments on David's celebration dance:

> For David, it was much more than a religious rite. It was the release from his remorse; the restoration of his joy in the Lord after profound repentance; the liberation of his whole person from fear of having offended the Almighty.
>
> In jubilation and pure adoration he began to leap and bound into the air with exhilaration. His poetic soul and artistic nature had to find full expression of gratitude in acknowledging that God,

very God, deigned once more to come and dwell among His people.[3]

## Michal's Response

Now in obedience to God, David was free. And whenever you're truly free, someone in the bondage of disobedience will envy your freedom—and will try to still your dance. David's wet blanket was his own wife Michal.

> Then it happened as the ark of the Lord came into the city of David that Michal the daughter of Saul looked out of the window and saw King David leaping and dancing before the Lord; and she despised him in her heart. . . .
> . . . When David returned to bless his household, Michal the daughter of Saul came out to meet David and said, "How the king of Israel distinguished himself today! He uncovered himself today in the eyes of his servants' maids as one of the foolish ones shamelessly uncovers himself!" (vv. 16, 20)

Michal's sarcastic, jealous jabs didn't sink David's joy. Caring more about God's opinion than hers, he defended his right to celebrate before his Lord.

> So David said to Michal, "It was before the Lord, who chose me above your father and above all his house, to appoint me ruler over the people of the Lord, over Israel; therefore I will celebrate before the Lord. And I will be more lightly esteemed than this and will be humble in my own eyes, but with the maids of whom you have spoken, with them I will be distinguished." (vv. 21–22)

As a consequence of her hatred toward David, Michal bore no children her whole life (v. 23). To a Jewish woman, the greatest curse was a barren womb.[4]

3. W. Phillip Keller, *David: The Shepherd King* (Waco, Tex.: Word Books, 1986), p. 55.

4. The issue is much more complex than Michal's simple irritation at her expressive husband. She was reflecting a fear of what the people might think instead of a fear of the Lord. It was that same preoccupation with image that got her father Saul into trouble. God may have prevented her from having children for three reasons: (1) to judge her for her attitude, (2) to stop the poisonous attitude from spreading from Saul, through her, to her children, and (3) to make sure that the house of Saul would have no possible claim to the throne.

## Lessons Learned

From David's episode with the ark, we learn two principles. First, *the better you know where you stand with the Lord, the freer you can be.* And second, *the freer you are before the Lord, the more confident you will become.*

When we disobey God, we may think we're free, but we're really in bondage—straight-jacketed by our own flesh and its sinful desires. But when we obey, we're free to enjoy a relationship with our Creator, free to fully express who He created us to be, and free to dance before Him in pure worship, unencumbered by the baggage of guilt and shame.

Have you discovered the freedom that comes with obeying God's will?

### *A Psalm of David*

*I will give thanks to the Lord with all my heart;*
*I will tell of all Thy wonders.*
*I will be glad and exult in Thee;*
*I will sing praise to Thy name, O Most High.*
(Ps. 9:1–2)

 *Living Insights*

According to the apostle Paul, the Lord said of His servant David, "'I have found David the son of Jesse, a man after My heart, *who will do all My will*'" (Acts 13:22, emphasis added).

Yet doing all of God's will didn't come naturally for David. He had to learn obedience, just as we do. When it comes to obeying God, it's often the details—the rings and poles—that snag us. Either we don't want to go to the trouble of getting the poles, or we don't want to carry them on our shoulders. So we grab a cart, rewrite the rules, and do it our own way.

When we disobey God's precepts, He may not strike us dead, as He did Uzzah, but His grief runs just as deep and His holiness is just as desecrated.

Are there some rings and poles you've been ignoring? Declaring every source of income at tax time . . . being kind to someone else's difficult child . . . honoring the authorities in your life?

David may not have done everything right all the time, but when he made a mistake, he had the humility to confess his sin and the courage to try again. How about you? Are you willing to pick up those poles and carry them according to *His* instructions? What do you need to do first?

_____

_____

_____

What's the next step?

_____

_____

_____

Wouldn't it be great to see God etch the same epitaph over our lives that He did over David's? He's not looking for perfection—He didn't find it in David, remember. He's just looking for a heart that is soft enough to love Him and humble enough to obey.

 ## Questions for Group Discussion

1. Ever try putting together a do-it-yourself kit without the instructions? You may start with good intentions, but you usually end up building an odd contraption that doesn't look anything like the picture. Paying attention to the details is important, especially in relating to God. Why do you think God's instructions for worshiping Him are so specific and unyielding?

2. What did David learn about God from his failed attempt to bring the ark to Jerusalem?

3. David's confession is noteworthy: "The Lord our God made an outburst on us, for we did not seek Him according to the ordinance"

(1 Chron. 15:13). Is it possible for a person to seek God while breaking His commands in the process? In what ways?

4. David was doubly exuberant when the ark finally arrived in Jerusalem because he was not only doing the right thing, he was doing it the right way. How does obeying God give you a sense of joy and freedom?

5. In David's response to Michal's criticism, he essentially said, "I'm not celebrating for your sake; I'm celebrating to please the Lord—and you ain't seen nothin' yet!" In what ways can you incorporate David's freedom and confidence into your own life?

## Chapter 14

# WHEN GOD SAYS NO

*2 Samuel 7*

On roads paved with praise, David had ushered the ark of God into Jerusalem. The procession had been his life's shining moment, and in the light of its glory, all the anguish and confusion from his past faded into a distant memory. The years of eating dust in the wilderness, the years of running like a hunted animal, the waiting . . . waiting . . . waiting had been worthwhile. Now all was well. The nation was enjoying a welcomed period of peace and rest, David was king, and the golden ark of God was safely in Jerusalem.

At that time, there was no temple. A tent—fabric, poles, and some rope—was all David had to offer the One who was his shield and protector, the Creator of the universe, the Almighty God. And that fact ate at David. The nation may have been at rest, but the king's mind was spinning with thoughts that would not go away.

## Personal Desire

As David compared his stately palace with the Lord's tent, he called for his trusted counselor, the prophet Nathan:

> "See now, I dwell in a house of cedar, but the ark of God dwells within tent curtains." (v. 2)

It didn't take a prophet to read David's mind. He was formulating a dream to build his Lord the grandest, most spectacular temple in the world. Sharing David's desire, Nathan assured him that his plan lined up with God's will.

> And Nathan said to the king, "Go, do all that is in your mind, for the Lord is with you." (v. 3)

However, Nathan spoke too soon.

## A Divine Response

In wanting to build God a temple, David's heart was in the right place. Yet, just because David's plan was noble and his friend was applauding it didn't mean it was God's will. It's a good idea to remember that every plan we may design *for* God isn't necessarily *of* God.

111

### Refusal of the Request

Nathan soon found out what the will of the Lord was—or shall we say, what it wasn't.

> And it came about the same night, that the word of God came to Nathan, saying, "Go and tell David My servant, 'Thus says the Lord, "You shall not build a house for Me to dwell in."'" (1 Chron. 17:3–4; see also 2 Sam. 7:4–7)

That was a hard message for Nathan to hear and even harder to pass on to the king. Later, David understood why God didn't want him to build His temple:

> "But the word of the Lord came to me, saying, 'You have shed much blood, and have waged great wars; you shall not build a house to My name, because you have shed so much blood on the earth before Me.'" (1 Chron. 22:8)

God's refusal wasn't a rejection of His faithful warrior but a redirection. He had a different plan for the king that neither Nathan nor David would ever have dreamed of.

### Plans for the Future

Speaking through Nathan, God told David:

> "'"I took you from the pasture, from following the sheep, that you should be ruler over My people Israel. And I have been with you wherever you have gone and have cut off all your enemies from before you; and I will make you a great name, like the names of the great men who are on the earth. I will also appoint a place for My people Israel and will plant them, that they may live in their own place and not be disturbed again, nor will the wicked afflict them any more as formerly, even from the day that I commanded judges to be over My people Israel; and I will give you rest from all your enemies. The Lord also declares to you that the Lord will make a house for you."'" (2 Sam. 7:8b–11)

God took away David's dream, it's true, and for an instant, the king's heart must have sunk. However, when the Lord told David *no*, He had a much greater *yes* behind it. The Lord gave David a covenant[1] that far outshined the privilege of building a temple.

### Covenant with the King

> """When your days are complete and you lie down with your fathers, I will raise up your descendant after you, who will come forth from you, and I will establish his kingdom. He shall build a house for My name, and I will establish the throne of his kingdom forever. I will be a father to him and he will be a son to Me; when he commits iniquity, I will correct him with the rod of men and the strokes of the sons of men, but My lovingkindness shall not depart from him, as I took it away from Saul, whom I removed from before you. And your house and your kingdom shall endure before Me forever; your throne shall be established forever.""" (vv. 12–16)

The "descendant" who would build the temple would be David's son Solomon, who was not yet born.[2] *Lovingkindness* is a special term in the Old Testament that refers to God's unconditional covenant blessing that He bestowed on Abraham, Isaac, Jacob, and was now giving to David and his dynasty. As a father to David's sons, God would stand firm against any disobedience, but He would never remove them from their place of favor with Him, like He removed Saul.[3]

Saul could have received God's promise of an everlasting kingdom, but he forfeited his future through his lack of faith (see

---

1. For an explanation of the Davidic covenant, see the Digging Deeper at the end of this chapter.

2. Solomon would be the second son born to David and Bathsheba. This is a remarkable testament to God's power and grace in working all things—including our sins, like David and Bathsheba's adultery, which was still future—together for the good He has planned (see Rom. 8:28).

3. Psalm 89 affirms the covenant God made with David, reminding the people that God will keep His promise, even though sometimes He seems to have abandoned them. "'My covenant I will not violate, Nor will I alter the utterance of My lips. Once I have sworn by My holiness; I will not lie to David. His descendants shall endure forever, And his throne as the sun before Me'" (vv. 34–36).

1 Sam. 13:13–14). David, however, in his passionate devotion to the Lord, proved himself worthy. Later, the Lord commended him,

> "'Because it was in your heart to build a house for
> My name, *you did well that it was in your heart.*'"
> (2 Chron. 6:8, emphasis added)

"God alone of all paymasters," writes Alexander Whyte, "pays as good wages for the good intentions of His servants as He pays for their best performances."[4] In return for wanting to make God's name great, God would make David's name great. And in response to David's dream of a stone-and-mortar house for God, God would build an eternal house for David—a dynasty that would lead all the way to the King of Kings, Christ himself. What an amazing display of grace!

## A Triumphant Prayer

Had David been the here-and-now type, the disappointment of God's *no* might have blinded him to the preciousness of God's promise. He might have become disillusioned and bitter—even jealous of his future son, who would accomplish what he couldn't.

Sometimes we focus so much on the privileges that God has given others that we overlook the priceless inheritance that He's laid in our laps. David didn't make that mistake. Overflowing with gratitude, he praised the God who had given him so much.

### Grateful Questions

Overwhelmed by God's goodness, David expressed his trust through a series of questions.

> "Who am I, O Lord God, and what is my house, that Thou hast brought me this far? And yet this was insignificant in Thine eyes, O Lord God, for Thou hast spoken also of the house of Thy servant concerning the distant future. And this is the custom of man, O Lord God. And again what more can David say to Thee? For Thou knowest Thy servant, O Lord God!" (2 Sam. 7:18b–20)

---

4. Alexander Whyte, *Bible Characters* (1952; reprint, Grand Rapids, Mich.: Zondervan Publishing House, 1959), vol. 1, p. 254

Then he showered the Lord with a fragrant sacrifice of praise and faith.

> "For this reason Thou art great, O Lord God; for there is none like Thee, and there is no God besides Thee, according to all that we have heard with our ears. And what one nation on the earth is like Thy people Israel, whom God went to redeem for Himself as a people and to make a name for Himself, and to do a great thing for Thee and awesome things for Thy land, before Thy people whom Thou hast redeemed for Thyself from Egypt, from nations and their gods? For Thou hast established for Thyself Thy people Israel as Thine own people forever, and Thou, O Lord, hast become their God. Now therefore, O Lord God, the word that Thou hast spoken concerning Thy servant and his house, confirm it forever, and do as Thou hast spoken, that Thy name may be magnified forever, by saying, 'The Lord of hosts is God over Israel'; and may the house of Thy servant David be established before Thee. For Thou, O Lord of hosts, the God of Israel, hast made a revelation to Thy servant, saying, 'I will build you a house'; therefore Thy servant has found courage to pray this prayer to Thee. And now, O Lord God, Thou art God, and Thy words are truth, and Thou hast promised this good thing to Thy servant. Now therefore, may it please Thee to bless the house of Thy servant, that it may continue forever before Thee. For Thou, O Lord God, hast spoken; and with Thy blessing may the house of Thy servant be blessed forever." (vv. 22a, 25–26a, 28–29)

David would spend the rest of his reign gathering materials, organizing workers, and drawing plans for a temple he would never build (see 1 Chron. 18:7–8; chaps. 22–26; 28–29). How he must have longed to stroll through the majestic halls and admire the immense columns, to run his fingers along the intricately carved stone and sing praises to His Lord in the golden sanctuary. Still, he was content. His son would build his Lord's temple and worship within its walls. And through his lineage, many more would come and worship, until, one day, the whole earth would be filled with the presence and the glory of God (see Hab. 2:14).

## Two Lasting Applications

Building a temple is probably not one of our secret ambitions, but all of us have dreams of how God will use our lives. Sometimes those hopes line up with God's will for us; sometimes they don't. When God says no to our plans, keep in mind a couple of principles.

First, *when God says no, He has a better way.* Look for the yes behind the no. God may not have any glorious temples for us to build, but there are always people around us who need building up. Often, God's yes will involve a son or daughter, a friend or neighbor. The legacy we leave behind, the values we build into our children, the lives we touch may be the greatest contributions we can make for God.

Second, *when God says no, our best reaction is humility and co-operation.* It takes real humility to say to the Solomons in your life, "You go, and may God be with you. I'll do everything I can to support you," and then sit back and applaud as they build your dream. What was David's secret of humility? Gratitude. He focused on what God had given him, not what He had taken away. And he never regretted the day when God said no.

### *A Psalm of David*

> *Bless the Lord, O my soul;*
> *And all that is within me, bless His holy name.*
> *Bless the Lord, O my soul,*
> *And forget none of His benefits;*
> *Who pardons all your iniquities;*
> *Who heals all your diseases;*
> *Who redeems your life from the pit;*
> *Who crowns you with lovingkindness and*
>     *compassion;*
> *Who satisfies your years with good things,*
> *So that your youth is renewed like the eagle.*
> (Ps. 103:1–5)

*Living Insights*

There was nothing wrong with David's dream to build the temple. His motives were pure; his intentions, pleasing to God. But he wasn't the right man to carry out the plan. God wanted a man of peace to build His temple.

Has God ever said no to one of your dreams? Perhaps you always wanted to go to the mission field, or maybe you desired to marry a godly person and raise children who love the Lord, or possibly you wanted to build a business based on Christian principles, or maybe . . . you fill in the blank. Yet God has closed every door you've tried to walk through.

This kind of mysterious no is hard to handle. But if we believe that God really loves us, really wants what's best for us—if we trust Him with our life—He will show us His better plan.

Where do you run when God tells you no? To the arms of disillusionment, or to the embrace of God?

_____

_____

_____

God does not call everybody to build "temples"—large, high-visibility achievements. Are you able to accept that fact? What makes it difficult?

_____

_____

_____

Referring to David's good intention to build the temple, God told him, "You did well that it was in your heart" (2 Chron. 6:8). Can you hear God's affirmation of your godly desires? What comfort and strength can you draw from it?

_____

_____

_____

As David supported Solomon, who would build his dream, how can you support others whom God may have called to fulfill your dream?

_____

_____

Broken dreams can shatter a person . . . but they don't have to. A spirit of gratitude for what God has given can help us release what He has taken away. What has God said yes to in your life? Try writing out some thoughts of gratitude to God, not necessarily to "count your blessings" but to express to Him a heartfelt willingness to accept His will for your life.

_____

_____

_____

 *Questions for Group Discussion*

1. Have you ever dreamed of God using your life in a special way? What was that dream?

2. "God doesn't call everybody to build temples." What does that statement mean to you?

3. God has given some people the privilege of doing great things for Him. Do you sometimes feel envious of those people, wishing God would use you that way?

4. God's no is not a discipline for sin or a rejection of you, but a redirection toward His will for your life. What do you think God's yes is for you?

5. David couldn't build the temple, but he could gather supplies and support the one whom God had chosen to build it. Does God want to fulfill your dream through someone else? How can you support that person?

6. Helping others succeed in a task you've always wanted for yourself is a true test of humility. Do you have a spirit of gratitude to God for what He's given you? Have you allowed him to foster genuine humility in your heart?

# 🛠 Digging Deeper

In *Explore the Book*, J. Sidlow Baxter calls the Davidic covenant in 2 Samuel 7 "one of the supremely great passages of the Bible, and one of the principal keys to the Divine plan of history."[5] In the immediate view, the promise refers to Solomon, who would build the temple, and David's lasting dynasty through the kings in Judah. But in a broader sense, the promise looks through the tunnel of time to David's greater Son, the Messiah, and the eternal kingdom of God.

According to Baxter, the Davidic covenant "marks a fourth major development in messianic prophecy."[6] The first covenant was with Adam, referring to the Messiah as the seed of the woman (Gen. 3:15); the second, to Abraham, identifying the messianic nation (see Gen. 22:18); the third, to Jacob, pinpointing his son Judah as the messianic tribe (see 49:10); and here, to David, re-vealing the messianic family.[7]

The prophets understood the significance of the promise, con-sistently teaching that the Messiah would come from David's line (see Isa. 9:6–7; 16:5; Jer. 23:5; Ezek. 37:24–25) and, specifically, from a virgin (Isa. 7:14; see also Matt. 1:22–23). Finally, when the Messiah was to be born, Gabriel affirmed that Mary's baby was the One whom Israel had been awaiting since David's day:

> "He will be great, and will be called the Son of the Most High; and the Lord God will give Him the throne of His father David; and He will reign over the house of Jacob forever; and His kingdom will have no end." (Luke 1:32–33)

The covenant guaranteed that three aspects of David's dynasty would endure forever: "(i) a 'house,' or posterity; (ii) a 'throne,' or royal authority; (iii) a 'kingdom,' or sphere of rule."[8] Today, we look forward to the time when Jesus Christ will fulfill these aspects of the covenant when He returns to establish His government on earth (see Isa. 11:1–10; Rev. 20:1–6; 21:1–5).

---

5. J. Sidlow Baxter, *Explore the Book*, 6 vols. in 1 (Grand Rapids, Mich.: Zondervan Publishing House, Academie Books, 1966), vol. 2, p. 73.

6. Baxter, *Explore the Book*, p. 75.

7. Baxter, *Explore the Book*, pp. 75–76.

8. Baxter, *Explore the Book*, p. 74.

## Chapter 15

# GRACE IN A BARREN PLACE
## 2 Samuel 9

A dancer's pirouette . . . people who carry themselves with charm and poise . . . a prayer given before a meal . . . music's most delicate notes. What do all these have in common? Each goes by the name *grace*.

Of all that this word identifies, though, its most significant meaning lies deep in the person of God.

Grace is God's snatching us from a barren place—a dry, desolate life of sin—and sitting us down to eat from the bounty of His table. It is undeserved and unrepayable. Best of all, it's free.

In 2 Samuel 9, we come to one of Scripture's richest illustrations of grace. Patterning his heart after God's by extending acceptance and mercy, David showers a shriveled soul with a refreshing rain of grace.

## An Example of Grace

The story begins years earlier with two promises David made— one to his dearest friend and the other to his bitterest enemy.

### Promises Made

The first promise was between David and Jonathan. Anticipating the day when David would become king, Jonathan had asked his friend in secret:

> "If I am still alive, will you not show me the lovingkindness of the Lord, that I may not die? And you shall not cut off your lovingkindness from my house forever, not even when the Lord cuts off every one of the enemies of David from the face of the earth." (1 Sam. 20:14–15)

In those days, an incoming king would hunt down and kill the deposed monarch's family to eliminate the possibility of retaliation or battle for the throne. David, however, vowed that he would spare

---

Portions of this chapter have been adapted from "Undeserving, Yet Unconditionally Loved," from the study guide *The Grace Awakening*, coauthored by Ken Gire, from the Bible-teaching ministry of Charles R. Swindoll, revised edition (Anaheim, Calif.: Insight for Living, 1996), pp. 33–35.

Jonathan and his family, showing them God's lovingkindness (v. 16).

The word *lovingkindness* in Hebrew is *chesed*, which can be translated "grace." Lovingkindness is the essence of *grace*—love expressed through kindness. Specifically, it is the demonstration of love toward those who don't deserve it and who can't repay.

David well understood the concept of grace. As an unknown shepherd boy, he had felt the oil of God's favor trickling down his face when Samuel anointed him. Ever since, God's grace had flowed through his life in an unending stream of protection and strength. Which brings us to the one he needed protection from.

The second promise was between David and Saul. Saul also knew in his heart that David would be king someday, and he pleaded with him,

> "Swear to me by the Lord that you will not cut off
> my descendants after me, and that you will not de-
> stroy my name from my father's household." (24:21)

In light of Saul's persecutions, David could have rightfully denied his request, but he graciously pledged to honor it instead (v. 22a).

Much had happened since David made those vows. Saul and Jonathan had been killed in battle. The nation had split, with Saul's son Ish-bosheth reigning in the north and David ruling in the south. Finally, Ish-bosheth had been assassinated by his own men. After years of waiting, David had ascended the throne of Israel and reached his zenith of power. The bright lights of success, however, didn't obscure his character. He was still a man of his word, and he wouldn't forget his promises.

### A Question Asked

> Then David said, "Is there yet anyone left of the
> house of Saul, that I may show him kindness for
> Jonathan's sake?" (2 Sam. 9:1)

"Kindness"—there's the Hebrew word again, *chesed*. His heart overflowing with grace, David asks for *anyone*—not just those who are worthy or qualified but anyone. His kindness is unconditional and free.

### An Answer Given

> Now there was a servant of the house of Saul whose

name was Ziba, and they called him to David. . . .
And Ziba said to the king, "There is still a son of
Jonathan who is crippled in both feet." (vv. 2a, 3b)

Perhaps unconsciously, Ziba hoists Jonathan's son's handicap as
a red flag. He tells the king nothing about the man, not even his
name—only that he is "crippled." Yet where Ziba sees a problem,
David sees a person. And where Ziba sees a deficiency, David sees
an opportunity for grace.

### A Son Sought

So the king said to him, "Where is he?" And Ziba
said to the king, "Behold, he is in the house of
Machir the son of Ammiel in Lo-debar." (v. 4)

Lo-debar means "no pasture." It refers to a wasteland. Incapable
of supporting himself and stripped of his inheritance, Jonathan's
son lives as an outcast in a barren place, far from the lush royal
estates that might have been his as Saul's grandson.

The last thing the former king's grandson wants to hear is an
emissary from King David rapping at his door. He doesn't know
why he's been summoned, but he must assume it is for execution.
Trembling, he hobbles into the king's chamber:

And Mephibosheth, the son of Jonathan the son of
Saul, came to David and fell on his face and pros-
trated himself. And David said, "Mephibosheth."
And he said, "Here is your servant!" (v. 6)

We finally discover the man's name: *Mephibosheth*. It means "one
who scatters shame."[1] He hadn't chosen his name, nor had he
chosen his life—which took a tragic turn the day his father and
grandfather were killed. Second Samuel 4:4 recounts the sad events
that marked his life forever:

Now Jonathan, Saul's son, had a son crippled in
his feet. He was five years old when the report of
Saul and Jonathan came from Jezreel, and his nurse
took him up and fled. And it happened that in her

---

1. Ronald F. Youngblood, *The Expositor's Bible Commentary*, 12 vols., gen. ed. Frank E.
Gaebelein (Grand Rapids, Mich.: Zondervan Publishing House, Academic and Professional
Books, 1992), vol. 3, p. 848.

hurry to flee, he fell and became lame. And his name
was Mephibosheth.

Ever since, Mephibosheth has borne the painful, disfiguring
reminder of that awful day. And now, as he lies prostrate before
David, he must fully expect to hear the whoosh of a sword on his
neck and to die as he has lived, in shame.

## The Result of Grace

The words that reach Mephibosheth's ears, however, are not
ones of judgment but of mercy.

> And David said to him, "Do not fear, for I will surely
> show kindness to you for the sake of your father
> Jonathan, and will restore to you all the land of your
> grandfather Saul; and you shall eat at my table regu-
> larly." (9:7)

Mephibosheth's parched soul can hardly absorb the grace that
David is showering on him.

> Again he prostrated himself and said, "What is your
> servant, that you should regard a dead dog like me?"
> (v. 8)

What has Mephibosheth done to merit such kindness? Nothing.
Had he deserved it, it wouldn't be grace. Grace is acceptance without reservation, forgiveness without condemnation, pardon without
probation. It is unrestrained love poured out on the undeserving.
And David isn't through pouring!

> Then the king called Saul's servant Ziba, and
> said to him, "All that belonged to Saul and to all
> his house I have given to your master's grandson
> [Mephibosheth]. And you and your sons and your
> servants shall cultivate the land for him, and you
> shall bring in the produce so that your master's
> grandson may have food; nevertheless Mephibo-
> sheth your master's grandson shall eat at my table
> regularly." Now Ziba had fifteen sons and twenty
> servants. Then Ziba said to the king, "According to
> all that my lord the king commands his servant so
> your servant will do." So Mephibosheth ate at David's

table as one of the king's sons. And Mephibosheth had a young son whose name was Mica. And all who lived in the house of Ziba were servants to Mephibosheth. So Mephibosheth lived in Jerusalem, for he ate at the king's table regularly. Now he was lame in both feet. (vv. 9–13)

The story ends here with a wonderful picture of Mephibosheth dining at the king's table, just like one of the king's own children. How sweet the taste of grace . . . and nobody knew the flavor better than Mephibosheth (see Ps. 34:8).

## Analogies of Grace

At least eight analogies connect David's grace to Mephibosheth with God's grace to us.

1. Once Mephibosheth had enjoyed fellowship with his father, and so had humanity in the Garden of Eden.

2. When disaster struck, fear came, and Mephibosheth suffered a fall that crippled him for the rest of his life. Similarly, when sin came, humanity suffered a fall, which has forever left us spiritually crippled.

3. Out of unconditional love for his friend Jonathan, David sought anyone to whom he might extend his grace. God, because of His unconditional love for His Son and acceptance of His Son's death on the cross, continues to seek anyone to whom He might extend His grace.

4. The crippled man was destitute and undeserving. All he could do was accept the king's favor. So, also, we sinners are undeserving and without hope. In no way are we worthy of our King's favor. All we can do is humbly and gratefully accept it.

5. The king took the crippled Mephibosheth from a barren wasteland and seated him at the royal banquet table in the palace. God, our Father, has rescued us from a moral wasteland and seated us in a place of spiritual nourishment and intimacy.

6. David adopted Mephibosheth into his royal family, providing him with every blessing within the palace. We also have been adopted into a family—God's family. And He gives us full privileges within His household.

7. Mephibosheth's limp was a constant reminder of David's grace. So also, our moral feebleness keeps us from ever forgetting that where sin abounds, grace abounds that much more.

8. When Mephibosheth sat at the king's table, he was treated with the same respect as David's own sons. When we one day attend the great wedding feast of the Lamb, the same will be true for us. We will sit with prophets and priests, apostles and evangelists, pastors and missionaries. We will dine with everyone from the apostle Peter to Corrie ten Boom. And we will be there with them because that same tablecloth of grace covers all our feet.

### A Psalm of David

*Thy lovingkindness, O Lord, extends to the heavens,*
*Thy faithfulness reaches to the skies.*
*Thy righteousness is like the mountains of God;*
*Thy judgments are like a great deep.*
*O Lord, Thou preservest man and beast.*
*How precious is Thy lovingkindness, O God!*
*And the children of men take refuge in the shadow of*
*     Thy wings.*
*They drink their fill of the abundance of Thy house;*
*And Thou dost give them to drink of the river of*
*     Thy delights.*
*For with Thee is the fountain of life;*
*In Thy light we see light.* (Ps. 36:5–9)

 *Living Insights*

Imagine the golden banquet hall of heaven.[2] The room radiates the glory of God. The doors open, and masses of people enter. But instead of the mighty and handsome, in hobble the sick, the lame, and the disfigured—those whose lives have been broken by the crippling effects of sin.

Take a moment to read Luke 14:15–24. When we were least worthy, God sent us an invitation, sealed by the blood of Christ,

---

2. This Living Insight is adapted from "The Classic Remedy," in the study guide *Classic Truths for Triumphant Living,* coauthored by Bryce Klabunde, from the Bible-teaching ministry of Charles R. Swindoll (Anaheim, Calif.: Insight for Living, 1996), pp. 23–24.

to dine at His royal table. He has snatched us from a barren place of sin and made us His princes and princesses. How does that knowledge change the way you see yourself?

_____

_____

_____

How does it alter the way you see others, particularly the outcast and the disabled?

_____

_____

_____

God's grace is so overwhelming, it's sometimes hard to put our gratitude into words. Perhaps the following poem can help you express your heart to the Lord.

### Grace in a Barren Place

I was that Mephibosheth
Crippled by my twisted pride and
 hiding from You in a barren place
  where You could not find me
  where You would not give me what I
   deserved

But somehow You found me and
I don't understand why but You
 gave me what I *do not* deserve
You not only spared my desolate life but
 You made it bountiful
And here at Your table
I will thank You my
 King.

—Julie Martin

## My Gratitude to God

_____

_____

_____

_____

_____

_____

_____

_____

_____

_____

 *Questions for Group Discussion*

1.  How would you define grace?

2.  Because of his family tie to Saul, Mephibosheth would have been considered an enemy of the throne. David had a right to kill him, but he was kind to him instead. List some of the ways David showed grace to Mephibosheth.

3.  Mephibosheth received favor based on the merit of another person—Jonathan. In what ways does Mephibosheth's story picture our salvation through Christ? See Galatians 4:4–7, Ephesians 2:4–9, and Titus 3:5–7.

4.  Mephibosheth's disability was a constant reminder of the tragic death of his father and his fall from fortune . . . *until* David showered him with grace. What did his handicap remind him of now? How might we view our "disabilities" in light of God's grace to us?

5.  We sometimes forget that God has made us princes and princesses and set us at His bountiful table. How can remembering God's grace influence the choices we make and our outlook on life?

## Chapter 16

# THE CASE OF THE OPEN WINDOW SHADE

*2 Samuel 11*

W hen the Holy Spirit portrays Scripture's heroes, He's a very realistic artist. He paints people just as they are, without airbrushing their faults or brightening their dark sides.

So far, we've seen the brilliant hues of David's faith and the somber colors of his failure. But now we come to the blackest part of the portrait—David's adultery with Bathsheba and its tragic aftermath.

We study this dark episode not to throw stones or shake our heads at David. Rather, we come to humbly learn. The Holy Spirit recorded this incident to warn us of sin's destructive power—even in those who love the Lord. As He admonished through the apostle Paul,

> Let him who thinks he stands take heed lest he fall.
> (1 Cor. 10:12)

## A Dark Backdrop

David is by now about fifty years old and has been king for about twenty years. He has welded Israel into a solid and powerful nation and distinguished himself as a mighty warrior, a gifted musician, a visionary man of God. Yet he is also like a seawall standing against a pounding sea of temptation. And the water is about to pour through his weakest points. His failure can be traced to three breaches.

### Polygamy and Lust

David may have been following the cultural norm for monarchs in his day, but by accumulating wives and concubines, he was violating God's higher standard. In Deuteronomy 17:17, God said that Israel's king should not "multiply wives for himself, lest his heart turn away."

Why did no one confront David about this sin? Perhaps they figured that his private life was his business. As long as the economy was expanding, the national defense was strong, and the country was healthy, what difference did his personal peccadilloes make?

But this seemingly harmless offense dug a wicked root into David's life. As his harem grew, so did his lust. The more a person indulges the sexual appetite, the more it increases. For David, this meant that even a houseful of women was not enough to keep his eyes from wandering.

### Vulnerability

David's military prowess had expanded his scope of power from the Euphrates River to the Red Sea. No enemy could stand against his mighty hand, for "the Lord helped David wherever he went" (2 Sam. 8:6b, 14b). Vassal kings brought him tribute, with money and honor flowing in like a river of gold.

Success, however, can be deceptively dangerous, particularly when we credit ourselves for it and get a swollen head. Never are we more vulnerable to the temptations of pride, self-indulgence, and unaccountability than when we have it all, and David was no exception.

### Indulgence

When his troops marched off to war, David did not share the hardships of battle with them but remained at Jerusalem (2 Sam. 11:1). Why did he stay behind? Maybe he felt that, after twenty years of trudging through battlefields, he deserved a rest. Besides, his soldiers were razor sharp, and Joab was more than capable of commanding them alone. So, while most kings were fighting alongside their men in battle, David cushioned himself in his palace, savoring the sweet wine of his success.

Susceptibility to lust, vulnerability to pride, and idleness. A dangerous combination—one that primed David for disaster.

## A Sensuous Scene

The scene opens in the royal bedroom, with David stirring from a late afternoon nap. The setting sun casts an amber glow across the evening sky. A warm spring breeze billows the curtains and swirls through his bedchamber. David yawns and stretches, his senses awakening to the perfume of the blossoming garden below. He slips on his robe and steps onto the palace balcony.

### Lurid Thoughts

Now when evening came David arose from his bed and walked around on the roof of the king's house, and from the roof he saw a woman bathing; and the woman was very beautiful in appearance. (v. 2)

Seeing the woman, he stops. He lingers. A glance becomes a gaze, a gaze stretches into a stare, a stare dissolves into a leer.

He loses all awareness of who he is or the danger that lies ahead. As the dense cloud of his aroused passion closes in around him, all he knows is the present. Everything else is forgotten—his family, his kingdom, even his God.

So David sent and inquired about the woman. And one said, "Is this not Bathsheba, the daughter of Eliam, the wife of Uriah the Hittite?" And David sent messengers and took her. (11:3–4a)

David's conscience is so numbed that his servant's warning about Bathsheba being married to one of the king's elite warriors doesn't even jab it awake (see 23:39; 1 Chron. 11:41). Within minutes, she is standing before him.

### Lustful Act

And when she came to him, he lay with her; and when she had purified herself from her uncleanness,[1] she returned to her house. (2 Sam. 11:4b)

The affair is brief. Some might call it a fling, a one-night stand, a fulfilled middle-aged fantasy. What's the harm? The problem is that David has violated God's Law. He has abused his power and broken the trust of his family.

Although he bears the heaviest blame, Bathsheba may bear some too. She could have resisted his advances or called out for help if she needed to. Instead, all that's recorded is silence on her part, implying willing cooperation.[2] Now they both must bear the consequences.

---

1. The King James and New International versions phrase this verse differently than the NASB. They show Bathsheba just having completed her ritual purification after her menstrual period (according to the Law—see Leviticus 15:19–33) *before* having relations with David. This would clearly show that she was not already pregnant before she came to him.

2. The Hebrew word for *lay* is *shakab*, meaning to rest or to lie down for sexual relations. Contrasted with this word is *anah*, which is the word for Amnon's rape of Tamar. There is no mention of force in David's tryst with Bathsheba.

### Lingering Result

> And the woman conceived; and she sent and told
> David, and said, "I am pregnant." (v. 5)

No doubt, David and Bathsheba's night of passion was exciting —
stolen waters are sweet. However, the consequences of sin are bitter,
and the taste will linger on their lips for a lifetime.

## A Panic Plan

Instead of facing his sin and confessing it before God and his
counselors, David panics and concocts a cover-up. For the first time
in his life, David tries to sweep his sin under the carpet, and in so
doing, he sells his precious integrity for a trash heap of hypocrisy
and deceit.

### Hypocrisy and Deception

> Then David sent to Joab, saying, "Send me
> Uriah the Hittite." So Joab sent Uriah to David.
> When Uriah came to him, David asked concerning
> the welfare of Joab and the people and the state of
> the war. Then David said to Uriah, "Go down to
> your house and wash your feet." And Uriah went
> out of the king's house, and a present from the king
> was sent out after him. (vv. 6–8)

It doesn't take X-ray vision to see through David's kindness
toward Uriah. He doesn't care about the war or the soldier; he only
cares about getting Uriah home to his wife. However, the king
doesn't count on the strength of this man's character.

Instead of going home to Bathsheba's waiting arms, Uriah sleeps
alongside David's servants at the palace door. When David asks him
why, he replies,

> "The ark and Israel and Judah are staying in tem-
> porary shelters, and my lord Joab and the servants
> of my lord are camping in the open field. Shall I
> then go to my house to eat and to drink and to lie
> with my wife? By your life and the life of your soul,
> I will not do this thing." (v. 11)

David, the commander in chief, is rebuked by the integrity of
a soldier—a man who is completely committed to the nation, to

his king, and to the Lord. As a last attempt at getting Uriah to go home to his wife, David wines and dines him until he is drunk. But even in a drunken state, Uriah displays more self-control than David. He refuses to go home (vv. 12–13).

### Violence and Murder

Panic-striken, David escalates his plan to the next level: murder. By Uriah's own hand, he sends Joab a message to put Uriah on the front lines of battle and abandon him where he will surely be killed (vv. 14–15). This time, the scheme works. Not only does Uriah die, but other soldiers die as well (v. 24).

## A Complete Cover-Up

Now David really has a mess to clean up. Not only must he conceal the adultery and the pregnancy but also the innocent blood on his hands.

### Before the Troops

When Joab sends word that the enemy has killed some soldiers and among the dead is Uriah, David replies with hypocritical consolation:

> Then David said to the messenger, "Thus you shall say to Joab, 'Do not let this thing displease you, for the sword devours one as well as another; make your battle against the city stronger and overthrow it;' and so encourage him." (v. 25)

### Before the Nation

David then moves to the final step in his scheme.

> Now when the wife of Uriah heard that Uriah her husband was dead, she mourned for her husband. When the time of mourning was over, David sent and brought her to his house and she became his wife; then she bore him a son. (vv. 26–27a)

Those closest to David must look on with a wary eye at the quick wedding and the early pregnancy. But when the baby is born early, their suspicions are confirmed. Still the matter is hushed, and the nation is deceived.

### But Not before God

David must have sighed with relief, thinking he got away with murder. However, God sees things differently.

> But the thing that David had done was evil in the sight of the Lord. (v. 27b)

With that sobering statement of God's justice, this dark chapter in David's life comes to an ominous close.

### A Psalm of David

> *The Lord is in his holy temple;*
>     *the Lord is on his heavenly throne.*
> *He observes the sons of men;*
>     *his eyes examine them. . . .*
> *For the Lord is righteous,*
>     *he loves justice.* (Ps. 11:4, 7a NIV)

 *Living Insights*

The fact that a godly man like David succumbed to such ungodly desires gives us much to consider. David's sin tell us a lot about . . .

- the power of our flesh
- the importance of renewing our devotion to God every day
- the danger of overindulging ourselves
- the power of sin to destroy our lives and the lives of those we love

Dietrich Bonhoeffer described what happens when our desires take control of our lives, as David's took control of his:

> At this moment God is quite unreal to us, he loses all reality, and only desire for the creature is real; the only reality is the devil. Satan does not here fill us with hatred of God, but with forgetfulness of God. . . . The lust thus aroused envelops the mind and will of man in deepest darkness. The powers of clear discrimination and of decision are taken from us.[3]

3. Dietrich Bonhoeffer, *Temptation* (1955; reprint, London, England: SCM Press, 1964), p. 33.

Bonhoeffer also says that our lusts can take many forms—"sexual desire, or ambition, or vanity, or desire for revenge, or love of fame and power, or greed for money."[4] Which form of lust is most likely to fill you with "forgetfulness of God" and steal your powers of "clear discrimination and decision"?

_____

_____

How can we control these desires? Scripture gives us two principles: first, "make no provision for the flesh in regard to its lusts" (Rom. 13:14b), and second, "flee from youthful lusts" (2 Tim. 2:22). Here are a few ways you can put these principles into action.

1. Establish boundaries that keep you out of compromising situations.[5]

2. Don't wait until you're tempted to weigh the consequences of your actions. Consider the consequences ahead of time.

3. Invite someone you trust to hold you to your standards.

4. Cultivate healthy pursuits that keep your thoughts on things that are honorable and pure and good (see Phil. 4:8).

5. Most importantly, cling to the Lord in daily dependence.

Specifically, what steps are you willing to take to protect yourself from lustful sins?

_____

_____

_____

_____

_____

_____

_____

4. Bonhoeffer, _Temptation_, p. 33.

5. An excellent book on this topic is _Loving Your Marriage Enough to Protect It_, by Jerry B. Jenkins, expanded edition (Chicago, Ill.: Moody Press, 1993).

 *Questions for Group Discussion*

1. If someone had told David as a young man that he would one day commit adultery, father an illegitimate child, and murder an innocent man, he would have exclaimed, "Never!" Yet it happened. Why do you think we are reluctant to believe we are capable of gross sin?

2. David's sin illustrates that godliness does not automatically protect us from temptation. In fact, temptations may increase the longer we walk with God. Is that thought disillusioning to you? How does it alter your definition of true godliness?

3. How does David's sin, in contrast to his position of favor with God, enrich your understanding of God's forgiveness and grace?

4. What do you think David could have done to protect himself against moral failure?

5. David's sin also shows us that we are never too old to sin. As long as our flesh is alive within us, we have the potential of committing the worst kinds of evil. What can you do to protect yourself against moral failure?

## Chapter 17

# CONFRONTATION!

*2 Samuel 12:1–15a*

D avid's sinful deed was done. The growing baby in his pregnant bride was now a mute reminder of that fateful spring night when adultery stained the king's record. Not only adultery but hypocrisy . . . and deception . . . and murder . . . and a cowardly cover-up.

No doubt, in the aftermath of David's crime, eyebrows were raised, two and two were put together, and scandalous whispers buzzed throughout the palace. But not one charge was laid against the king, not one finger of judgment pointed his way. Even so, David was hardly free. A far harsher prosecutor kept him bound in a straitjacket of guilt—his conscience. The Greek philosopher, Polybius, once said,

> There is no witness so dreadful, no accuser so terrible as the conscience that dwells in the heart of every man.[1]

And David was feeling the full scorn of his accuser.

## Twelve Months in Retrospect

For about a year, David lived in misery. He conducted the same affairs of state as before, met with the same people, kept the same schedule. Externally, nothing changed; yet on the inside, everything changed. The memory of his sin hounded him during the day and haunted him at night. In Psalm 51, he wrote, "For I know my transgressions, And my sin is ever before me" (v. 3).

Riddled with guilt, David began to deteriorate physically. Listen to his suffering in this psalm:

> When I kept silent about my sin, my body wasted
>> away
> Through my groaning all day long.
> For day and night Thy hand was heavy upon me;

---

1. Polybius, as quoted in *Bartlett's Familiar Quotations*, 15th ed., rev. and enl., ed. Emily Morison Beck (Boston, Mass.: Little, Brown and Co., 1980), p. 95.

My vitality was drained away as with the fever
heat of summer. (Ps. 32:3–4)

Nothing, however, compared to the agony of the silence from
God. For perhaps a full year, the heavens were shut against David;
God's flaming sword guarded the gates of fellowship. For the first
time, David knew what it was like to feel hopelessly, desperately,
utterly alone.

These are the wages that sin pays. Despite his suffering, David
hardened his heart and refused to confess his sin, until . . .

## One Moment of Truth

In 2 Samuel 12, God penetrated David's prideful defenses
through the bold confrontation of the prophet Nathan.

### Sent by God

The chapter begins with a simple but important word, *then*. God
waited until just the right time, after Bathsheba's baby had been
born, after sin's misery had softened him sufficiently. *Then* He
stepped in (v. 1a).

### Encounter with the King

Wisely, Nathan didn't burst in shouting accusations at the king.
God wanted David restored, not shot down. So the Lord sent
Nathan with a parable designed to touch David's heart.

> "There were two men in one city, the one rich
> and the other poor.
> The rich man had a great many flocks and herds.
> But the poor man had nothing except one little
> ewe lamb
> Which he bought and nourished;
> And it grew up together with him and his children.
> It would eat of his bread and drink of his cup
> and lie in his bosom,
> And was like a daughter to him.
> Now a traveler came to the rich man,
> And he was unwilling to take from his own flock
> or his own herd,
> To prepare for the wayfarer who had come to him;

Rather he took the poor man's ewe lamb and
　　prepared it for the man who had come to him."
(vv. 1b–4)

The story stirred David's own memories of being a poor shepherd and how he had loved his sheep. It also unleashed emotions he had bound and gagged in his efforts to live with his guilt—emotions such as compassion, zeal for justice, anger at evil.

Nathan knew his parable had worked when David exploded with rage:

> Then David's anger burned greatly against the man, and he said to Nathan, "As the Lord lives, surely the man who has done this deserves to die. And he must make restitution for the lamb fourfold, because he did this thing and had no compassion." (vv. 5–6)

The Law required the rich man to pay back four sheep for the one he stole (see Exod. 22:1; Luke 19:8), but that punishment was too lenient for the rich man. Because he was so coldly indifferent to the poor man, when he had so many lambs of his own to choose from, David said he deserved death. In passing judgment on the rich man, David had issued his own sentence.

Quickly, Nathan unsheathed the sharp-edged words of truth and plunged them into David's heart: "You are the man!" (2 Sam. 12:7a)

In chastened silence, David listened to Nathan expose the dark details of his sin as revealed by God.

> "Thus says the Lord God of Israel, 'It is I who anointed you king over Israel and it is I who delivered you from the hand of Saul. I also gave you your master's house and your master's wives into your care, and I gave you the house of Israel and Judah; and if that had been too little, I would have added to you many more things like these! Why have you despised the word of the Lord by doing evil in His sight? You have struck down Uriah the Hittite with the sword, have taken his wife to be your wife, and have killed him with the sword of the sons of Ammon.'"[2] (vv. 7b–9)

2. David had broken three of the Ten Commandments—"you shall not covet your neighbor's wife," "you shall not commit adultery," and "you shall not murder" (Exod. 20:13–14, 17).

Although pained by Nathan's lancing words, David must have felt a gush of relief. Finally, the festering sins were in the open. No more living a lie. No more pretending nothing was wrong. But there would be consequences to face. Through Nathan, the Lord continued,

> "'Now therefore, the sword shall never depart from your house, because you have despised Me and have taken the wife of Uriah the Hittite to be your wife.' Thus says the Lord, 'Behold, I will raise up evil against you from your own household; I will even take your wives before your eyes, and give them to your companion, and he shall lie with your wives in broad daylight. Indeed you did it secretly, but I will do this thing before all Israel, and under the sun.'"
> (vv. 10–12)

The rule of restitution was enacted against David. The sword of violence he had used against Uriah would pierce his own family.[3] And the private affair he had had with Bathsheba would be multiplied in public by another man, who would have an affair with not just one but many of his wives.

### Repentance and Restoration

> Then David said to Nathan, "I have sinned against the Lord." (2 Sam. 12:13a)

David's words were few, but as commentators Keil and Delitzsch point out,

> "That is a good sign of a thoroughly broken spirit. . . . There is no excuse, no cloaking, no palliation of the sin. There is no searching for a loophole, . . . no pretext put forward, no human weakness pleaded. He acknowledges his guilt openly, candidly, and without prevarication."[4]

---

3. Some commentators see the deaths of Bathsheba's baby and David's sons Amnon, Absalom, and Adonijah as the fulfillment of the fourfold restitution required in the Law (see Exod. 22:1). See Ronald F. Youngblood, "2 Samuel," in *The Expositor's Bible Commentary*, gen. ed. Frank E. Gaebelein (Grand Rapids, Mich.: Zondervan Publishing House, Academic and Professional Books, 1992), vol. 3, p. 943.

4. C. F. Keil and F. Delitzsch, *Commentary on the Old Testament*, 2 vols. in 1 (reprint; Grand Rapids, Mich.: William B. Eerdmans Publishing Co., 1976), vol. 2, p. 391.

David had used Bathsheba, betrayed Uriah, shamed his family, and disgraced the nation; but he had sinned against the Lord. When David finally admitted it, even though he deserved death, God showed him grace:

> And Nathan said to David, "The Lord also has taken
> away your sin; you shall not die." (v. 13b)

However, to protect his Name, God would take the life of David's illegitimate son so that the Lord's enemies would have no reason to blaspheme (v. 14). With the last of the judgments given, the confrontation was over, and Nathan went home (v. 15).

## Advice to Apply

Through Nathan's confrontation, David's broken relationship with God was mended. Let's take a moment to study the specifics of confrontation and repentance so that we can keep sin from shattering the spirits of others and ourselves.

### Confrontation

From Nathan's example, we pick up four principles to remember when we are called to confront.

First, *base the charges on absolute truth*. Take time to get all the facts before you point your finger.

Second, *wait for God's timing*. Confronting a person too early, while emotions are turbulent, can do more harm than good. Better to wait for God's go-ahead. "Like apples of gold in settings of silver Is a word spoken in right circumstances" (Prov. 25:11).

Third, *use wise wording*. Nathan didn't accuse David right away; he softened his heart with a word picture. Plan your words carefully before you talk to the person.

Fourth, *go with courage*. No one likes to be confronted. We always run the risk of straining a relationship or even losing a friend. But the risk is well worth the reward when the person is restored. "Faithful are the wounds of a friend" (Prov. 27:6).

### Repentance

David's example shows us what true repentance involves:

- an open, unguarded admission of guilt
- a desire to make a complete break from the sin

- a broken and humble spirit

- a claiming of God's forgiveness and reinstatement

After the confrontation, David penned perhaps one of his most moving psalms—a psalm embodying an attitude of genuine repentance. Listen to his words. Hear the cry of his broken spirit. And you will know the heart of a man truly sorry for his sin.

### A Psalm of David

> Be gracious to me, O God, according to Thy
>     lovingkindness;
> According to the greatness of Thy compassion blot
>     out my transgressions.
> Wash me thoroughly from my iniquity,
> And cleanse me from my sin. . . .
> Against Thee, Thee only, I have sinned,
> And done what is evil in Thy sight,
> So that Thou art justified when Thou dost speak,
> And blameless when Thou dost judge. . . .
> Purify me with hyssop, and I shall be clean;
> Wash me, and I shall be whiter than snow.
> Make me to hear joy and gladness,
> Let the bones which Thou hast broken rejoice.
> Hide Thy face from my sins,
> And blot out all my iniquities.
> Create in me a clean heart, O God,
> And renew a steadfast spirit within me.
> Do not cast me away from Thy presence,
> And do not take Thy Holy Spirit from me.
> Restore to me the joy of Thy salvation,
> And sustain me with a willing spirit.
> Then I will teach transgressors Thy ways,
> And sinners will be converted to Thee.
> (Ps. 51:1–2, 4, 7–13)

*Living Insights*

If David lived today, he might have tried one of the following methods to ease his troubled conscience.

- Rationalizing: "What's one sin compared to a lifetime of good living? Everybody makes mistakes. God will understand."

- Shifting the blame: "It's Bathsheba's fault! If she hadn't been bathing in plain view, I would never have fallen for her, and Uriah would be alive today."

- Justifying: "Bathsheba wasn't happy with Uriah. Actually, getting rid of him was the best thing I could have done for her."

- Making excuses: "I was really depressed when all that happened. How can I be responsible for what I did?"

- Skirting the issue: "What I did is nothing compared to what Saul did. Now *he* was a real reprobate."

- Legitimizing: "Most men have at least one affair during their lifetime. It's normal."

- Intellectualizing: "How does anyone know right from wrong? What's wrong for you may not be wrong for me."

Do any of these look familiar? Which do you sometimes use, and why?

_____

_____

David's method was to keep silent about his sin (Ps. 32:3). He refused to talk about his deed—just swept it away as if it never happened. (That's not easy to do with the fruit of his sin growing larger every day inside his pregnant wife.) Why didn't—and doesn't—this method work? Have you tried this method?

_____

_____

_____

There's only one way to ease a guilty conscience: *repentance*. That involves (1) getting your sin out in the open, confessing it; (2) asking forgiveness; (3) restoring your relationship with the person you offended (including God); and (4) paying restitution, if needed.

For most people, repentance doesn't come easy. It took Nathan's stern confrontation to get David to do it. But when he did, a feeling of relief washed over David like a clear fountain of spring water.

> How blessed is he whose transgression is forgiven,
> Whose sin is covered!
> How blessed is the man to whom the Lord does
>     not impute iniquity,
> And in whose spirit there is no deceit! (Ps. 32:1–2)

You don't have to live with a guilty conscience. In His mercy, God has provided you with a way to freedom through the waters of repentance. Let Him cleanse you today.

 *Questions for Group Discussion*

1. Reread the seven methods from the Living Insight that David could have used to ease his troubled conscience. Which ones do you hear most often today?

2. Have you used any of them? Which ones?

3. Have you ever followed David's example and just kept quiet about your sin? If so, how has that affected your life?

4. Why do you think God waited a full year before sending Nathan to confront David?

5. What do you learn from Nathan about confronting someone?

6. Using Nathan's and David's examples, how would you help a person move from improperly handling their sin to repentance and restoration?

## Chapter 18

# TROUBLE AT HOME

*Selected Scriptures*

W hen storms rage, the best place to be is home, protected
from the howling winds and the cold, rainy blasts. . . .
Unless the blizzard is inside the home.

Chill winds from cold hearts and pounding tempests of rebellion
can devastate a family like no amount of rain or snow ever could.
For when we've been careless about our relationships with the Lord
and others, we learn firsthand what the prophet Hosea declared:

> For they sow the wind,
> And they reap the whirlwind. (8:7a)

Kings are no exception to this principle, as David would find
out. He had sown the wind with Bathsheba, and he was about to
reap the whirlwind.

Before we look at the tragic repercussions that tore apart David's
home, let's get a firmer grasp on the stark, enduring truth Hosea
recorded. It applies not just to David but to us as well.

### Principle from Scripture

The apostle Paul stated Hosea's principle a little more directly
in Galatians 6.

> Do not be deceived, God is not mocked; for what-
> ever a man sows, this he will also reap. For the one
> who sows to his own flesh shall from the flesh reap
> corruption. (vv. 7–8a)

We will reap in like kind what we have sown (only magnified).
If we sow sin, even after we confess it and restore our communion
with God, we must live with the consequences—the broken trust,
the painful memories, the bruised reputation, the fractured hearts.
The pain of the reaping always eclipses the pleasure of the sowing.

God is still with us as we endure our consequences. In fact, He
often uses them to restore and redirect and redeem our lives. As
Paul said when he finished verse 8:

> But the one who sows to the Spirit shall from the
> Spirit reap eternal life. (v. 8b)

David's repentance truly restored him to God. His promised dynasty would still last for centuries, and the Messiah would still come through him. In David's life, "where sin increased, grace abounded all the more" (Rom. 5:20b). However, his one night of ecstasy and subsequent murder plot produced sorrow and regret for many years to come.

## Problems in the Palace

Nathan had forecasted the pain David would have to endure in one simple but scathing pronouncement:

> "'Now therefore, the sword shall never depart from your house.' . . . Thus says the Lord, 'Behold, I will raise up evil against you from your own household.'"
> (2 Sam. 12:10a, 11a)

We can trace the line of David's sin with Bathsheba to eight consequences that led him on a downward path of grief and heartache.

### 1. David and Bathsheba's Newborn Son Dies

Nathan had told David, "Because by this deed you have given occasion to the enemies of the Lord to blaspheme, the child also that is born to you shall surely die" (v. 14). And so it happened.

> Then the Lord struck the child that Uriah's widow bore to David, so that he was very sick. David therefore inquired of God for the child; and David fasted and went and lay all night on the ground. And the elders of his household stood beside him in order to raise him up from the ground, but he was unwilling and would not eat food with them. Then it happened on the seventh day that the child died.
> (vv. 15b–18a)

What had this baby done to deserve death? Nothing. Often, the innocent ones suffer the most for our selfish choices. Had David and Bathsheba only taken a moment to consider the effect their sin would have on the little life their adultery might produce, they might have restrained their desires.

### 2. Amnon Rapes Tamar

Like a black shadow, the consequences of David's sin next stretched across his firstborn son, Amnon, and daughter Tamar.

Now it was after this that Absalom the son of
David had a beautiful sister whose name was Tamar,
and Amnon the son of David loved her. (13:1)

But it was the wrong kind of love. It wasn't affectionate, broth-
erly love. It was physical and incestuous.

And Amnon was so frustrated because of his sister
Tamar that he made himself ill, for she was a virgin,
and it seemed hard to Amnon to do anything to her.
(v. 2)

Taking the counsel of Jonadab, a wicked friend, Amnon feigned
sickness to get his half sister Tamar to care for him in his bed.
When she brought him something to eat,

he took hold of her and said to her, "Come, lie with
me, my sister." But she answered him, "No, my
brother, do not violate me, for such a thing is not
done in Israel; do not do this disgraceful thing!"
(vv. 11b–12)

Refusing to listen to Tamar, he raped her (v. 14). And his "love"
for her immediately showed itself for what it truly was: hatred.

Then Amnon hated her with a very great hatred;
for the hatred with which he hated her was greater
than the love with which he had loved her. And
Amnon said to her, "Get up, go away!" (v. 15)

### 3. Absalom Hates Amnon

When Absalom, Tamar's full brother, found out about the rape,
the domestic storm whipped up into a seething fury.

But Absalom did not speak to Amnon either good
or bad; for Absalom hated Amnon because he had
violated his sister Tamar. (v. 22)

How did David, the judge of the nation and protector of his
home, respond to the jolting news of Tamar's rape and Absalom's rage?

Now when King David heard of all these matters,
he was very angry. (v. 21)

That's all. Sadly, David's anger went no further. Maybe the king
felt unworthy to judge Amnon because of his own track record of

lust. Even so, Tamar desperately needed her father to come to her aid, to vindicate her through swift and severe justice. Yet David did nothing. Was she worth so little that Amnon could abuse her and get away with it? If David wouldn't restore her dignity, her brother, Absalom, would—with a sword.

### 4. Absalom Murders Amnon

Absalom waited two years for David to act (v. 23). But because of his father's passivity, Absalom's hatred festered into a plot to murder Amnon.

> And Absalom commanded his servants, saying, "See now, when Amnon's heart is merry with wine, and when I say to you, 'Strike Amnon,' then put him to death." . . . And the servants of Absalom did to Amnon just as Absalom had commanded. (13:28a, 29a)

### 5. Absalom Rebels and Runs Away

After David heard about Amnon's death, Absalom fled to the home of his grandfather—Talmai, king of Geshur (vv. 37–39). There he remained as a refugee for three years, with no contact from David in all that time. In effect, David had now lost three sons.

### 6. Absalom Leads a Conspiracy

Joab sent for a woman from Tekoa to convince the king to pardon Absalom and bring him home to Jerusalem (14:1–23). David, however, followed up his amnesty for Absalom with this order:

> "Let him turn to his own house, and let him not see my face." So Absalom turned to his own house and did not see the king's face. (v. 24)

David may have given Absalom the finest house to live in, money to spend, and servants to meet his needs, but he didn't give him the one thing his son needed most: a relationship with his father.

Shoved aside for two more years (v. 28), Absalom began to loathe his father and determined to take the precious kingdom David had spent his life building. In the four years that followed, Absalom "stole away the hearts of the men of Israel" (15:6b). When a messenger told David of his son's conspiracy, David became afraid:

> "Arise and let us flee, for otherwise none of us shall

escape from Absalom. Go in haste, lest he overtake us quickly and bring down calamity on us and strike the city with the edge of the sword." (15:14b)

### 7. Absalom Violates David's Wives

The Lord had warned David through Nathan that just as he had taken another man's wife, so another man—someone close to him—would take his wives and lay with them, not secretly, but in broad daylight before all Israel (see 12:11b–12). Now we find this prediction fulfilled by David's own son.

So they pitched a tent for Absalom on the roof, and Absalom went in to his father's concubines in the sight of all Israel. (16:22)

Notice where Absalom pitched his shameful tent. On the palace roof—the very place where David had sown the wind of adultery.

### 8. Joab Murders Absalom

The whirlwind came to its tragic culmination with Absalom's death. As he was riding his mule, he became caught in the low branches of a great oak. The mule bolted, leaving him hanging by his long, thick hair. Although given explicit orders to spare him, Joab took advantage of Absalom's vulnerable position.

So he took three spears in his hand and thrust them through the heart of Absalom while he was yet alive in the midst of the oak. (18:14b)

When David got word of his son's death, years of regret and pent-up feelings broke forth in a torrent of tears.

And the king was deeply moved and went up to the chamber over the gate and wept. And thus he said as he walked, "O my son Absalom, my son, my son Absalom! Would I had died instead of you, O Absalom, my son, my son!" (v. 33)

## Final Thoughts

As the sun set that evening, David's mournful wail drifted through the city, like the plaintive toll of a funeral bell. And it tolls today as a somber warning to us all. David's grief calls to the spouse allured by the fantasy of a secret affair, to the parent drawn to a busy life that leaves no room for the children, to any person tempted to exchange his or her future for the fleeting pleasures of sin. Are the selfish choices that we so casually cast to the wind worth the whirlwind that waits to strike us and those we love?

If you've begun to veer into the path of carnality, thinking that you can do what you want and God's grace will cover your tracks, stop and think again. Although grace cancels the debt of sin, it doesn't necessarily cancel the consequences of sin. God's forgiveness is sure, but so is sin's harmful fallout. Ask yourself, "How many innocent people will suffer in the wake of my sin?" How David wished he had asked himself that question before he called for Bathsheba. Sadly for him, the warning came too late. But for us, it may be just in time.

### A Psalm of David

*O Lord, do not rebuke me in Thine anger,*
*Nor chasten me in Thy wrath.*
*Be gracious to me, O Lord, for I am pining away;*
*Heal me, O Lord, for my bones are dismayed.*
*And my soul is greatly dismayed;*
*But Thou, O Lord—how long?* (Ps. 6:1–3)

 *Living Insights*

The best time to brace your house against a storm is before the rain starts falling and the wind begins to howl. Likewise, the best time to protect yourself against the stormy consequences of sin is before temptation strikes.

If David had only considered the whirlwind his sin would cause *before his passions were aroused,* he might never have sown the wind of adultery with Bathsheba. Now, while the winds are calm, ask yourself a few hard questions about what might happen if you were to fail morally.

Who would my moral failure injure?

_____

_____

_____

_____

How would my sin impact my reputation?

_____

_____

_____

My ministry?

_____

_____

_____

My career?

_____

_____

_____

What devastation would my sin cause my family?

_____

_____

_____

How would my sin change my relationship with God?

_____

_____

_____

_____

Can any pleasure be worth this much pain?

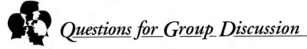 *Questions for Group Discussion*

1. Do you agree or disagree with this statement: "People today get away with sin more than people in our parents' generation did"?

2. Do you think the consequences of sin have changed much over the years?

3. What consequences never change?

4. We sometimes use the following statements in the midst of temptation to convince ourselves that it's OK to sin. What errors of thinking can you find in them?

    "If I play it smart, I can have the best of both worlds."
    "If I keep my sin secret, no one will get hurt."
    "Even if I get caught, I can always ask forgiveness."

5. How can David's tragic example help safeguard you against a future moral fall?

6. Share your answers to the Living Insights questions on the previous page. What's the common thread running through the answers?

## Chapter 19

# RIDING OUT THE STORM

*2 Samuel 12:15b–25*

It's midnight; Rockport, Maine. The harbor is quiet, except for the boats' creaking decks and the water slapping up against the wooden hulls. Within minutes, though, storm clouds begin to tumble through the sky. Thunder rumbles; rain pelts. The tranquil little harbor is tossed by a whirlwind.

One boat, tied loosely to its moorings, snaps its rope and is carried out by the violent currents to crash upon the rocks.

But another boat—secured to the dock and firmly anchored— rides out the storm and is ready to sail when the sun comes out in the morning.

Our last chapter showed David in the center of the whirlwind, reaping the results of his sin. In this chapter, we'll see how he weathered the storm—whether he sank or survived—and why. We'll see that when the waves of sin's consequences begin to slosh the decks of our lives, our only hope for survival is to anchor ourselves to the Lord.

## David's Confession of the Sowing

"'I have sinned against the Lord'" (2 Sam. 12:13). The simple confession that poured from David's heart had spoken to God with more eloquence than any ornate prayer. At once, God graciously released him from the death penalty the Law demanded (see Exod. 21:12, 14; Lev. 20:10). Now David stood clean before the Lord, forgiven and restored. He had escaped God's penal judgment . . . however, he hadn't escaped God's paternal discipline.

In the Davidic covenant, the Lord had made a promise concerning David's son that would apply to him as well:

> "'"I will be a father to him and he will be a son to Me; when he commits iniquity, I will correct him with the rod of men and the strokes of the sons of men."'" (2 Sam. 7:14)

God's chastisement was meant to correct David, not punish him. It was designed to show him how serious sin is to a holy God and to protect him from future moral failure.[1]

How did David respond to God's discipline? In the same way that he confessed his sin: with humility and trust in God.

## David's Response to the Reaping

Nathan told David that the first gust of the whirlwind would be the death of his infant son (12:14). With that dire prediction, David had to decide how to react. Like the boat that was loosed from its moorings, his life could have ended up broken on the rocks of bitterness. But instead, he dropped four anchors of faith that helped him ride out the storm.

### He Prayed

When the baby suddenly became ill, David's first response was prayer.

> Then the Lord struck the child that Uriah's widow bore to David, so that he was very sick. David therefore inquired of God for the child; and David fasted and went and lay all night on the ground. And the elders of his household stood beside him in order to raise him up from the ground, but he was unwilling and would not eat food with them. (vv. 15b–17)

God's discipline was painful; but rather than running *from* God, David ran *to* Him. In his prayers, he quieted himself before the Lord, pleading for the life of his son. It was a soul-searching time for David, a time to be alone and consider the gravity of his offense. An innocent child was suffering because of him. As long as there was a chance that God might spare the child, David would pray feverishly to that end. Just maybe . . .

### He Faced the Consequences Realistically

After seven days, however, the infant died. David's servants

---

1. Unlike punishment, discipline is forward-looking. Chrysostom wrote, "[God] imposes a penalty upon us—not to punish us for past sins, but to correct us against future ones." In *Calvin: Institutes of the Christian Religion*, ed. John T. McNeill, The Library of Christian Classics (Philadelphia, Pa.: Westminster Press, 1960), vol. 1, p. 662.

were afraid to tell him, concerned that, in the depths of his sorrow, he might take his own life (v. 18). But David's response was surprisingly calm.

> When David saw that his servants were whispering together, David perceived that the child was dead; so David said to his servants, "Is the child dead?" And they said, "He is dead." So David arose from the ground, washed, anointed himself, and changed his clothes; and he came into the house of the Lord and worshiped. (vv. 19–20a)

Instead of blaming himself more, he put himself back together and went to worship God. The baby was dead, and he couldn't change that. He could, however, accept what he had received from God's hand and humbly bow before Him, knowing that God was both merciful and just.

### He Claimed God's Truths

His servants were astonished at his response! "What is this thing that you have done?" they asked,

> "While the child was alive, you fasted and wept; but when the child died, you arose and ate food." (v. 21)

David's answer reveals that he had secured his hope in the sovereignty of God.

> And he said, "While the child was still alive, I fasted and wept; for I said, 'Who knows, the Lord may be gracious to me, that the child may live.' But now he has died; why should I fast? Can I bring him back again? I shall go to him, but he will not return to me." (vv. 22–23)

David's response shows that he believed God was in control not only of his destiny but also his son's. His son was gone, but one day he would see him again. Even in the midst of his suffering, David relied on God's truth.

### He Went On, Refusing to Give Up

After the funeral and after mourning his loss with his wife, David found the grace to live again.

Then David comforted his wife Bathsheba, and went in to her and lay with her; and she gave birth to a son, and he named him Solomon. Now the Lord loved him and sent word through Nathan the prophet, and he named him Jedidiah for the Lord's sake. (v. 24–25)

It takes God's grace to endure the whirlwind, but it also takes God's grace to move on once the storm has calmed.

## Observations to Be Made

Along with the guidelines we've studied, several general observations can be made about riding out the storm.

First, *it's a lonely experience*. We will never be more alone than when we are in the whirlwind of sin's consequences. Others may want to help, but we alone will experience the depth of our pain.

Second, *it's a learning experience*. God can use the storm to reveal a side of ourselves that we've never seen before. He can also show us aspects of His character—His justice, His sovereignty, His holiness, and His grace.

Third, *it's a temporary experience*. We may feel like it will last forever, but it won't. It will end. God's power will see us through.

Finally, *it's a humbling experience*. Look at what Moses wanted the Israelites to remember from their wilderness wanderings:

"And you shall remember all the way which the Lord your God has led you in the wilderness these forty years, that He might humble you, testing you, to know what was in your heart. . . . And He humbled you and let you be hungry." (Deut. 8:2a, 3a)

When we're going through the whirlwind, our lives won't be fruitful. We will be enduring a harsh, barren time. To humble us, God will let us be hungry for His blessings—because He values a contrite heart.

### A Psalm of David

*For Thou dost not delight in sacrifice, otherwise I
would give it;
Thou art not pleased with burnt offering.
The sacrifices of God are a broken spirit;
A broken and a contrite heart, O God, Thou wilt
not despise. (Ps. 51:16–17)*

*Living Insights*

Are you riding out the stormy consequences of sin? Perhaps, in the past, you sowed the wind of rebellion, selling your godly principles for a taste of fleshly pleasures. And now, you're reaping the whirlwind. Violent waves are crashing over you and straining your moorings. Everything you hold dear is slipping from your hands— the trust of your family, your reputation, your self-respect. You've confessed your sin, but there are still consequences to endure. What do you do?

Or maybe you're riding out someone else's storm. A son, daughter, spouse, or friend has sowed the wind, and now *you* are suffering the consequences. They may not comprehend what their sin is doing to you—they may not even care—but you're drowning in the wake of their sinful lifestyle. What do you do?

In both situations, David's responses to God's discipline provide some guidelines.

### 1. He Prayed

In your pain, have you been pushing God away, running from Him instead of to Him? If so, take some time now to draw near to Him, even if it's to express your doubts and confusion.

### 2. He Faced the Consequences Realistically

When nothing can be changed, it's time to let it go. Are you still beating yourself up over past mistakes? Have you let the guilt of old sins shrink the boundaries of your future and your hope? What does God's forgiveness of David teach you about forgiving yourself?

_____

_____

_____

### 3. He Claimed God's Truths

David anchored himself to certain truths, such as God's sovereignty, the hope of heaven, and God's love for us even during times of discipline. What truths do you need to hang on to?

_____

### 4. He Went On, Refusing to Give Up

Sometimes we can focus so much on what we've lost that we forget about what we have. Bitterness and regret over yesterday's pain can rob us of today's joy. What has God given you today, to take part in or to love?

Whether you're riding out your own storm or someone else's, remember that God is not punishing you. As a father disciplines his children, He wants to correct you, not condemn you; to strengthen you, not sink you. Don't be afraid to anchor yourself to Him.

## Questions for Group Discussion

1. When you were a child, were you punished or disciplined? In your opinion, what is the difference between the two?

2. When you were caringly disciplined, how did you respond? Were you open to it or resentful of it?

3. How have you accepted discipline as an adult?

4. Every trial is not necessarily God's discipline. Job lost his children, but unlike David, he had done nothing wrong. How can you know if your trial is discipline or testing?

5. Review the four ways David handled God's discipline. What do you learn from his example that will help you endure the consequences of sin in your life or someone else's life?

    a. He prayed
    b. He faced the consequences realistically
    c. He claimed God's truths
    d. He went on, refusing to give up

# Chapter 20
# FRIENDS IN NEED
### 2 Samuel 15; 17:27–29; 19:1–8

Samuel Taylor Coleridge was a melancholy genius. Born in 1772 in Devonshire, England, his brilliance shone at an early age. In his twenties, he penned his masterpiece *The Rime of the Ancient Mariner* and published it in a book of poems with his good friend William Wordsworth. They titled the collection *Lyrical Ballads*, and critics consider that collaborative work "a landmark in English literature and the beginning of nineteenth century Romanticism."[1]

Despite the promise of his early success, however, his life did not fare so well. By the time he reached thirty, he had begun using opium to temper the pain from his rheumatism. As a result, he became addicted—and desperate. In time, his marriage fell apart and his longtime friendship with Wordsworth ran aground after a bitter quarrel. Still hopelessly gripped by his drug addiction, Coleridge was now without family or friend. It was his darkest, loneliest hour—"A grief without a pang, void, dark, and drear."[2]

In 1816, a sympathetic physician named James Gillman came to Coleridge's aid and managed to help him control his opium habit. Eventually, the poet renewed his rich friendship with Wordsworth and came to an amiable understanding with his wife. His room at Highgate became a center for literary repartee; and by the end of his life, the "Sage at Highgate" was entertaining a regular stream of eager disciples and good friends.

A man of great talent and even greater troubles, Coleridge understood the value of friendship. In his reflective poem *Youth and Age*, he wrote: "Friendship is a sheltering tree."[3]

Like those great, green trees whose leafy limbs shelter us from the sun's hot rays, friends provide refuge when adversity beats down on us. Everyone needs the shelter of friends, and David was no

1. *Cyclopedia of World Authors*, rev. ed., ed. Frank N. Magill, (Englewood Cliffs, N.J.: Salem Press, 1974), p. 388.

2. Samuel Taylor Coleridge, "Dejection: An Ode," in *Library of the World's Best Literature*, ed. Charles Dudley Warner (New York, N.Y.: R. S. Peale and J. A. Hill Publishers, 1897), vol. 7, p. 3838.

3. Samuel Taylor Coleridge, "Youth and Age," in *Poems That Live Forever*, comp. Hazel Felleman (New York, N.Y.: Doubleday, 1965), p. 256.

exception. In this chapter, we'll see him during the period prior to and just after Absalom's death, in desperate need of "sheltering trees," and we'll learn some essential things about friendship from those who stood faithfully by his side.

## The Needs in David's Life

Because of his tragic season of moral compromise, David needed shelter and support for three reasons. *Personally*, he was awash in guilt from his adultery and murder. *Domestically*, his family had been devastated by death, rape, revenge, and rebellion. *Politically*, he was losing control of his kingdom as his ambitious son Absalom maneuvered himself into power. Second Samuel 15:2–6 describes Absalom's shrewd strategy.

> Absalom used to rise early and stand beside the way to the gate; and it happened that when any man had a suit to come to the king for judgment, Absalom would call to him and say, "From what city are you?" And he would say, "Your servant is from one of the tribes of Israel." Then Absalom would say to him, "See, your claims are good and right, but no man listens to you on the part of the king." Moreover, Absalom would say, "Oh that one would appoint me judge in the land, then every man who has any suit or cause could come to me, and I would give him justice." And it happened that when a man came near to prostrate himself before him, he would put out his hand and take hold of him and kiss him. And in this manner Absalom dealt with all Israel who came to the king for judgment; so Absalom stole away the hearts of the men of Israel.

Having undermined his father's authority, Absalom took the next step in his mutinous plot.

## The Crisis to Withstand

Absalom traveled to Hebron under the pretense of paying a vow to the Lord—ironically, David's last words to his son were, "Go in peace" (v. 9). From Hebron (where his father had first been crowned king), Absalom sent spies throughout the country to quietly spread the conspiracy. A trumpet blast would be the signal that Absalom was the new king of Israel (v. 10).

The plan worked, with village after village swinging their support behind him. When some of David's loyalists felt the tremors of insurrection, they reported the news to the king: "The hearts of the men of Israel are with Absalom" (v. 13). To avoid a bloody civil war, David had no choice but to abandon Jerusalem to his rebel son and run for his life.

He quickly gathered his belongings, his family, and his private guard and started his exodus. With the hot Palestinian sun of hardship beating down on him, David now more than ever needed friendship's sheltering tree.

## The People Who Stood Near

To meet David's needs, God provided him not just one friend but a "grove" of faithful supporters.

### Ittai

The first friend came to David as he paused at the eastern edge of Jerusalem. David was letting his company cross the brook Kidron ahead of him when he noticed someone he didn't expect to see: Ittai the Gittite. Ittai was a Philistine official from Gath who had recently defected to Israel. He was already a displaced person. Why would he involve his family and his men in more uncertainty by following David (v. 19)? The king urged him to return:

> "You came only yesterday, and shall I today make you wander with us, while I go where I will? Return and take back your brothers; mercy and truth be with you." (v. 20)

In contrast to David's own countrymen, Ittai vowed his loyalty to the king.

> But Ittai answered the king and said, "As the Lord lives, and as my lord the king lives, surely wherever my lord the king may be, whether for death or for life, there also your servant will be." (v. 21)

Now that's a true friend. When everyone else has turned away, there will be a few who will say, "I'm with you. Count on me. I'm here to the end." One might even be a person from Gath—a person who had been your enemy, but who has come full circle to become your friend. Blood ties don't always guarantee friendship. David's son became an enemy while, ironically, a Philistine proved to be his friend.

### Zadok and Abiathar

Following Ittai and his men were the priests Zadok and Abiathar and a company of Levites carrying the ark of the covenant (v. 24). The ark symbolized God's favor, which surely was with David and not Absalom. David, however, wasn't comfortable making that assumption. He asked Zadok and Abiathar to return the ark and wait for God to act:

> "If I find favor in the sight of the Lord, then He will bring me back again, and show me both it and His habitation. But if He should say thus, 'I have no delight in you,' behold, here I am, let Him do to me as seems good to Him." (vv. 25b–26)

Once again, David showed himself a man after God's heart by surrendering himself completely to God's will. Whether under the hand of discipline or blessing, David determined to let God have His way with him.

For Zadok and Abiathar, two faithful supporters of David, returning to Jerusalem might have meant hardship and even death. Yet as good friends, they were willing to do as he requested, with no argument (v. 29).

### Hushai

Once David's company had crossed the brook Kidron, he led the mournful procession up the Mount of Olives. It was a heart-wrenching scene. The great king of Israel "wept as he went, and his head was covered and he walked barefoot" (v. 30).

Waiting for him at the summit was Hushai the Archite, wearing signs of empathy—a torn robe and dust on his head (v. 32). A servant, advisor, and friend, Hushai planned to accompany David in his exile. But David had another plan in mind for Hushai: espionage.

> And David said to him, "If you pass over with me, then you will be a burden to me. But if you return to the city, and say to Absalom, 'I will be your servant, O king; as I have been your father's servant in

time past, so I will now be your servant,' then you can thwart the counsel of Ahithophel for me.[4] . . . So it shall be that whatever you hear from the king's house, you shall report to Zadok and Abiathar the priests. Behold their two sons are with them there, Ahimaaz, Zadok's son and Jonathan, Abiathar's son; and by them you shall send me everything that you hear." (vv. 33–36)

Without question, and without being offended that David chose not to take him along, Hushai returned to join Absalom's court as a spy (v. 37; see also 16:15–19). As it turned out, he played a key role in saving David's life and kingdom.

After Absalom took over Jerusalem, Ahithophel urged the young king to attack David right away, while he was exhausted from fleeing (17:1–4). Had Absalom taken his advice, he would have trapped his father at the Jordan River and destroyed him. But, as God planned it, Absalom followed Hushai's advice to wait before attacking (vv. 5–14a).

> For the Lord had ordained to thwart the good counsel of Ahithophel, in order that the Lord might bring calamity on Absalom. (v. 14b)

Secretly, Hushai sent word to David to hurry across the Jordan into the wilderness. The messengers, Jonathan and Ahimaaz, were almost caught, but God protected them when a woman hid them in a well (vv. 15–20). David received the warning and escaped to Mahanaim, where three more friends stepped in to help (vv. 21–24a).

### Shobi, Machir, and Barzillai

Anticipating the condition of David and his men, Shobi, Machir, and Barzillai offered them a cool cup of hospitality.

> Now when David had come to Mahanaim, Shobi the son of Nahash from Rabbah of the sons of Ammon, Machir the son of Ammiel from Lodebar, and Barzillai the Gileadite from Rogelim, brought beds, basins, pottery, wheat, barley, flour,

---

4. Ahithophel, once David's sagacious counselor, had defected to Absalom. Ahithophel's words were highly regarded: "the advice of Ahithophel, which he gave in those days, was as if one inquired of the word of God" (2 Sam. 16:23).

parched grain, beans, lentils, parched seeds, honey, curds, sheep, and cheese of the herd, for David and for the people who were with him, to eat; for they said, "The people are hungry and weary and thirsty in the wilderness." (vv. 27–29)

Without being asked, these generous friends furnished the refugees with water, supplies, a place to stay, and the best food in town.[5] That's what friends do. They don't hold back when you're in need. And their kindness restores your spirit and puts you on your feet again.

### Joab

David hit the bottom of his despair when Absalom died. A thrust of a spear had ended the rebellion; but for David, the regret was just beginning. Weeping and moaning, David cried out his dead son's name over and over, "O my son Absalom, my son, my son Absalom!" (v. 33). How he wished that the spear had been rammed through his own heart . . . yet, in a sense, it had. It took a man like Joab to bring David back to the land of the living.

> And the king covered his face and cried out with a loud voice, "O my son Absalom, O Absalom, my son, my son!" Then Joab came into the house to the king and said, "Today you have covered with shame the faces of all your servants, who today have saved your life and the lives of your sons and daughters, the lives of your wives, and the lives of your concubines, by loving those who hate you, and by hating those who love you. For you have shown today that princes and servants are nothing to you; for I know this day that if Absalom were alive and all of us were dead today, then you would be pleased. Now therefore arise, go out and speak kindly to your servants, for I swear by the Lord, if you do not go out, surely not a man will pass the night with you, and this will be worse for you than all the evil that has come upon you from your youth until now." (19:4–7)

5. Each of these men had good reason *not* to help David. Shobi's people—the Ammonites— were David's enemies. Machir from Lo-debar had done his share by taking in Jonathan's son, Mephibosheth (2 Sam. 9:4–5). And Barzillai was eighty years old. He could have considered himself retired and sent someone younger (19:32).

Joab dared to confront David, which is what a good friend must sometimes do. The king's tears were drowning his sensitivity to the people who had risked their lives to save him. And they were demoralized (v. 3). It was too late now to open his heart to Absalom. But David's people were there, and they needed his leadership in Jerusalem.

## Some Final Thoughts

As we reflect on the people who came to David's rescue during his darkest hours, we come away with some truths about friends.

First, *friends are essential.* There is no substitute for a friend— someone to care, to listen, to comfort, and even to reprove (see Prov. 27:6, 17).

Second, *friends must be cultivated.* As one man has written, "If a man does not make new acquaintances as he advances through life, he will soon find himself left alone. A man, sir, should keep his friendship in a constant repair."[6]

Third, *friends impact our lives.* Those we are close to rub off on us, change us. Their morals and philosophies, convictions and character eventually become our own (see 1 Cor. 15:33; Prov. 13:20).

Fourth, *friends can be one of four types.* They can be an acquaintance, a casual friend, a close friend, or an intimate friend—which is the closest of all. You have the fewest number of intimate friends, but you also enjoy the highest level of honesty with them. These are the people with whom you have regular contact and a deep commitment to mutual character development. With them, you share the freedom to criticize and correct, encourage and embrace.

### A Psalm of David

*Behold, how good and how pleasant it is*
*For brothers to dwell together in unity!*
*It is like the precious oil upon the head,*
*Coming down upon the beard,*
*Even Aaron's beard,*
*Coming down upon the edge of his robes.*
*It is like the dew of Hermon,*
*Coming down upon the mountains of Zion;*
*For there the Lord commanded the blessing—life forever.*
(Ps. 133:1–3)

6. Samuel Johnson, as quoted in *Bartlett's Familiar Quotations,* 15th ed., rev. and enl., ed. Emily Morison Beck (Boston, Mass.: Little, Brown and Co., 1980), p. 354.

*Living Insights*

Who are your "sheltering trees"? If you were in need, whose refuge would you run to?

_____

_____

_____

Friendships like these are rare and precious . . . and easy to take for granted. What can you do to cultivate your friendships before hardships come?

_____

_____

_____

It's true, the best way to make friends is to be a friend. Is there a despairing "David" in your life who needs your shelter? Who is this person?

_____

David's friends encouraged him in unique ways. Which of them can you use for a model as you help your friend?

❏ *Ittai*, who gave a vow of loyalty

❏ *Zadok and Abiathar*, who gave spiritual support

❏ *Hushai*, who worked on David's behalf

❏ *Shobi, Machir, and Barzillai*, who gave material support

❏ *Joab*, who gave a needed reproof

What shelter do you plan to provide for your friend?

_____

_____

_____

The greatest model of friendship is Jesus Christ. When we were His enemies, rebellious and proud, He covered us with His canopy of grace and offered His life for ours (see John 15:13; Rom. 5:8). Each time you shelter a friend, you show Christ's love. Your hand of kindness becomes His hand; your words of encouragement, His words; your touch of mercy, His touch. Like Him, you become a sheltering tree.

## Questions for Group Discussion

Imagine that you are the successful president of a Fortune 500 corporation. After a falling out with your son, he forms a rival company and begins stealing your clients. One day, your staff tells you that all your customers have closed their accounts and the company is bankrupt. A few days later, your creditors attach liens to your property and bank accounts. You are left penniless. But ruining you is just the beginning; your son has determined to kill you! Now you must run for your life.

1. If this were happening to you, what feelings would you be dealing with?

2. How did David cope with his son's betrayal and rebellion?

3. Each of David's friends offered him a different kind of shelter. What did Ittai give? Zadok and Abiathar? Hushai? Shobi, Machir, and Barzillai? Joab?

4. Think back through your life. Have you had a friend who was a "sheltering tree" to you? What did he or she do that was especially helpful?

5. Not one person met all of David's needs. They all helped according to their abilities, and together they supported him. Think about someone you know who is enduring the sweltering heat of hardship (maybe even someone in the group). What unique shelter do you have to offer this person?

## Chapter 21

# BEING BIG ENOUGH TO FORGIVE

*2 Samuel 16:5–13; 19:16–23*

*I forgive you.* Few words hold as much power to heal the human spirit as these. Freely given, they can mend a broken friendship or breathe life into a dying marriage. They can be the first rays of sunlight to a soul imprisoned in guilt or the first sign of rescue to a sinner lost in a sea of regret.

Many people, however, struggle with the words. The heart does not easily release them, and when it does, they often come out tangled with ulterior motives. Sometimes the forgiveness is *conditional*—"I will forgive you, if . . ." Other times the forgiveness is *partial*—"I'll forgive, but I won't ever forget." Still other times the forgiveness is *delayed*—"I'll forgive you, but not right now."

Truly forgiving is hard to do. But if we don't forgive, we set ourselves on a downhill path toward further heartache and pain. What begins as an offense leads to

      resentment . . .

        then hatred . . .

          then a grudge . . .

          and finally bottoms out at revenge.

Only one person consistently resisted the pull of that destructive path and forgave completely—Jesus Christ. Even the pressure of the Cross and the malice of His enemies could not squeeze one ounce of bad blood from His heart. When they pounded the hateful nails into His flesh, only love poured out of His veins: "Father, forgive them; for they do not know what they are doing" (Luke 23:34).

In the scene from David's life that we're about to study, David faces a hurtful situation in which he, too, must decide to forgive. In one sense, he passed the test with flying colors. But in another, he fell short of perfect forgiveness, for he was only human. In him, we find an example of a man who struggled with forgiveness and who can encourage us in our own struggles.

## An Example of Forgiveness

The story begins in the midst of David's flight from Jerusalem.

Having just lost the throne to his own son, David trudges wearily along the dusty road. With each step, he feels the weight of his grief bearing down on him, crushing him with regret and sorrow. Into this scene of personal tragedy enters a vile vulture of a man who comes to feed on David's disgrace.

### Shimei's Offense

> When King David came to Bahurim, behold, there came out from there a man of the family of the house of Saul whose name was Shimei, the son of Gera; he came out cursing continually as he came. And he threw stones at David and at all the servants of King David; and all the people and all the mighty men were at his right hand and at his left. And thus Shimei said when he cursed, "Get out, get out, you man of bloodshed, and worthless fellow! The Lord has returned upon you all the bloodshed of the house of Saul, in whose place you have reigned; and the Lord has given the kingdom into the hand of your son Absalom. And behold, you are taken in your own evil, for you are a man of bloodshed!" (2 Sam. 16:5–8)

Notice that this man Shimei is a relative of Saul. He has probably nursed a grudge against David for more than twenty years, ever since the royal dynasty shifted to David's house. His vision blurred by hatred, Shimei sees David's calamity as God's judgment for his "sin" against Saul . . . and as a chance to take some sweet revenge.

Shimei's charges are untrue, however. David didn't murder Saul, neither did he steal Saul's throne. And God didn't give Absalom the throne—he took it!

Few offenses plunge deeper into our flesh than false accusations, particularly when they're hurled at us when we're vulnerable. Abishai, one of David's right-hand men,[1] rises hotly to his master's defense, and forgiveness is the farthest thing from his mind.

> Then Abishai the son of Zeruiah said to the king, "Why should this dead dog curse my lord the king? Let me go over now, and cut off his head." (v. 9)

---

1. Abishai, Joab, and Asahel (who was killed many years before by Saul's general, Abner) were David's nephews, sons of his sister Zeruiah (see 1 Chron. 2:12–16).

David, however, fixes his eyes on God instead of Shimei. Through the hailstorm of lies, one statement penetrates David's conscience with a measure of truth: David *is* a man of bloodshed. He killed Uriah. Thinking that Shimei's curses may be part of God's discipline for that heinous deed, David restrains Abishai.

> "What have I to do with you, O sons of Zeruiah? If he curses, and if the Lord has told him, 'Curse David,' then who shall say, 'Why have you done so?'" Then David said to Abishai and to all his servants, "Behold, my son who came out from me seeks my life; how much more now this Benjamite? Let him alone and let him curse, for the Lord has told him. Perhaps the Lord will look on my affliction and return good to me instead of his cursing this day." So David and his men went on the way; and Shimei went along on the hillside parallel with him and as he went he cursed, and cast stones and threw dust at him. (vv. 10b–13)

### Shimei's Confession

In the days that follow, the Lord does "return good" to David. He thwarts Absalom's rebellion and restores David to the throne. He picks up the story in 2 Samuel 19, where the king is triumphantly returning to Jerusalem. Suddenly, Shimei shows up with a thousand men from his tribe (vv. 16–18), this time singing a different tune.

> So he said to the king, "Let not my lord consider me guilty, nor remember what your servant did wrong on the day when my lord the king came out from Jerusalem, so that the king should take it to heart. For your servant knows that I have sinned; therefore behold, I have come today, the first of all the house of Joseph to go down to meet my lord the king." (vv. 19–20)

Shimei's blasphemies against the Lord's anointed were a capital offense, a fact that Abishai zealously points out:

> "Should not Shimei be put to death for this, because he cursed the Lord's anointed?" (v. 21b)

Abishai-type people delight in the letter of the law and in watching people get what they deserve. Their advice is always, Fight back! Make him pay! To them, showing mercy is a sign of weakness. To David, however, showing mercy is a sign of strength and the cornerstone of his restored government.

> David then said, "What have I to do with you, O sons of Zeruiah, that you should this day be an adversary to me? Should any man be put to death in Israel today? For do I not know that I am king over Israel today?" And the king said to Shimei, "You shall not die." Thus the king swore to him. (vv. 22–23)

How could David show such restraint? Two reasons. First, his focus was on the Lord—he had left Shimei's offense in God's hands (16:12). Second, he was aware of his own failure. Once he had stood in Shimei's shoes, crying out, "I have sinned," and God had forgiven him for crimes much worse than hurling insults at a king. How could he *not* forgive Shimei?

## A Sobering Ending

As much as we would like the story to end here, with the tender strains of forgiveness ringing in the air, it doesn't. It concludes years later, on David's deathbed. In his final instructions to Solomon, David's open hand of mercy toward Shimei tightens into a fist.

> "And behold, there is with you Shimei the son of Gera the Benjamite, of Bahurim; now it was he who cursed me with a violent curse on the day I went to Mahanaim. But when he came down to me at the Jordan, I swore to him by the Lord, saying, 'I will not put you to death with the sword.' Now therefore, do not let him go unpunished, for you are a wise man; and you will know what you ought to do to him, and you will bring his gray hair down to Sheol with blood." (1 Kings 2:8–9)

How tragic that the sweet singer of Israel should approach his final days with revenge on his lips. As great a man as David was, as great an example, as great a king, he was still very much human. And, as Alexander Whyte explains, that's a point we can all take to heart.

> David at his best, as at his worst, is one of ourselves. David is a man of like passions with ourselves. David

was cut out of the same web, and he was shaped out of the same substance as ourselves. He was a man of like passions with us, and, like our passions, his were sometimes at his heel, but more often at his throat. David held back his bad passions at Saul, and at Shimei, and at Joab, occasion after occasion, till we were almost worshipping David. But, all the time, and all unknown to us, they were there. Till, of all times and of all places in the world, David's banked-up passions burst out on his deathbed, that no flesh might glory in God's presence.[2]

## Some Practical Suggestions

David's experience reminds us how hard it is to truly forgive. It's also a somber warning to keep a vigilant watch over our hearts for the sprouting seeds of resentment. The following suggestions can help you stop yourself at the offense level, before a grudge has a chance to grow.

First, *develop a thicker layer of skin.* We can become so sensitive to criticism that we fret over every little comment that people make about us. The slightest pinprick mortally wounds our self-esteem. We need to ask the Lord to give us tougher skin—to make us confident enough in Him and ourselves that we can ignore criticisms that we know aren't true.

Second, *try to understand where your offender is coming from.* Look beyond the offense to the hurting person lashing out. People don't always mean what they say; we may just happen to be a convenient target for their pent-up frustrations. By showing love and concern for the person in return, we can help them see the real issue, and we can turn a hurtful conflict into an opportunity for healing (see Prov. 12:18).

Third, *recall times in your life when you have needed forgiveness.* "Just as the Lord forgave you, so also should you" (Col. 3:13). Forgiven people make the best forgivers.

Finally, *openly declare forgiveness, and go on from there.* The words "I forgive you" are the best therapy for both the offender and the offended. If you've been offended, free yourself and the one who has hurt you with a verbal gift of grace. Don't let past injuries silence your song for the Lord.

2. Alexander Whyte, *Bible Characters,* (1952; reprint, Grand Rapids, Mich.: Zondervan Publishing House, 1959), vol. 1, p. 252.

## A Psalm of David

*He has not dealt with us according to our sins,*
*Nor rewarded us according to our iniquities.*
*For as high as the heavens are above the earth,*
*So great is His lovingkindness toward those who fear*
*    Him.*
*As far as the east is from the west,*
*So far has He removed our transgressions from us.*
*Just as a father has compassion on his children,*
*So the Lord has compassion on those who fear Him.*
*For He Himself knows our frame; He is mindful that*
*    we are but dust.*
(Ps. 103:10–14)

 *Living Insights*

In his fable "The Magic Eyes," Lewis Smedes illustrates the power and the miracle of forgiveness.

> In the village of Faken in innermost Friesland there lived a long thin baker named Fouke, a righteous man, with a long thin chin and a long thin nose. Fouke was so upright that he seemed to spray righteousness from his thin lips over everyone who came near him; so the people of Faken preferred to stay away.
>
> Fouke's wife, Hilda, was short and round, her arms were round, her bosom was round, her rump was round. Hilda did not keep people at bay with righteousness; her soft roundness seemed to invite them instead to come close to her in order to share the warm cheer of her open heart.
>
> Hilda respected her righteous husband, and loved him too, as much as he allowed her; but her heart ached for something more from him than his worthy righteousness.
>
> And there, in the bed of her need, lay the seed of sadness.
>
> One morning, having worked since dawn to knead his dough for the ovens, Fouke came home

and found a stranger in his bedroom lying on Hilda's round bosom.

Hilda's adultery soon became the talk of the tavern and the scandal of the Faken congregation. Everyone assumed that Fouke would cast Hilda out of his house, so righteous was he. But he surprised everyone by keeping Hilda as his wife, saying he forgave her as the Good Book said he should.

In his heart of hearts, however, Fouke could not forgive Hilda for bringing shame to his name. Whenever he thought about her, his feelings toward her were angry and hard. . . . When it came right down to it, he hated her for betraying him after he had been so good and so faithful a husband to her.

He only pretended to forgive Hilda so that he could punish her with his righteous mercy.

But Fouke's fakery did not sit well in heaven.

So each time that Fouke would feel his secret hate toward Hilda, an angel came to him and dropped a small pebble, hardly the size of a shirt button, into Fouke's heart. Each time a pebble dropped, Fouke would feel a stab of pain. . . .

The pebbles multiplied. And Fouke's heart grew very heavy with the weight of them, so heavy that the top half of his body bent forward so far that he had to strain his neck upward in order to see straight ahead. Weary with hurt, Fouke began to wish he were dead.

The angel who dropped the pebbles into his heart came to Fouke one night and told him how he could be healed of his hurt.

There was one remedy, he said, only one, for the hurt of a wounded heart. Fouke would need the miracle of the magic eyes. He would need eyes that could look back to the beginning of his hurt and see his Hilda, not as a wife who betrayed him, but as a weak woman who needed him. . . .

Fouke protested. "Nothing can change the past," he said. "Hilda is guilty, a fact that not even an angel can change."

"Yes, poor hurting man, you are right," the angel

said. "You cannot change the past, you can only heal the hurt that comes to you from the past. And you can heal it only with the vision of the magic eyes."

"And how can I get your magic eyes?" pouted Fouke.

"Only ask, desiring as you ask, and they will be given you. And each time you see Hilda through your new eyes, one pebble will be lifted from your aching heart."

Fouke could not ask at once, for he had grown to love his hatred. But the pain of his heart finally drove him to want and to ask for the magic eyes that the angel had promised. So he asked. And the angel gave.

Soon Hilda began to change in front of Fouke's eyes, wonderfully and mysteriously. He began to see her as a needy woman who loved him instead of a wicked woman who betrayed him.

The angel kept his promise; he lifted the pebbles from Fouke's heart, one by one, though it took a long time to take them all away. Fouke gradually felt his heart grow lighter; he began to walk straight again, and somehow his nose and his chin seemed less thin and sharp than before. He invited Hilda to come into his heart again, and she came, and together they began again a journey into their second season of humble joy.[3]

Are pebble-sized thoughts of resentment weighing your heart down? If so, who hurt you?

_____

How is your heavy heart changing your disposition? Your spiritual life?

_____

_____

_____

3. Lewis B. Smedes, _Forgive and Forget: Healing the Hurts We Don't Deserve_ (New York, N.Y.: Simon and Schuster, Pocket Books, 1984), pp. 13–15.

Are you willing to ask Christ for a pair of "magic eyes"—the eyes of His love—through which you can see your offender from a new perspective? Or have you grown to love your hatred?

_____

_____

God can do many things for you. He can lift the pebbles from your heart. He can help you heal your hurt. But there's one thing He can't do—He can't undo the past. Can you live with that?

To forgive someone doesn't mean we have to "forget" the offense entirely. That's impossible. Forgetting has more to do with restoring an injured relationship, with letting the pain slowly fade until it doesn't ache whenever you see the other person. It's learning to trust again. It's accepting the past and leaving it behind rather than dragging it into the future.

Forgiveness is not a snap-of-the-fingers miracle. It's a journey that involves work, commitment, faith, and time to heal. But the God of forgiveness will be with you every step of the way, strengthening you on your journey to becoming more like the ultimate forgiver, His Son.

 *Questions for Group Discussion*

1. Lewis Smedes wrote, "When you forgive the person who hurt you deeply and unfairly, you perform a miracle that has no equal."[4] What do you think his statement means? How is forgiveness a miracle?

2. An unforgiving spirit can lead to resentment, hatred, grudges, and revenge. Have you witnessed this downward process in others? In yourself?

3. Shimei's words were like knives, stabbing David in the heart. What was so painful about Shimei's accusations?

4. Was Abishai wrong to desire that Shimei get what he deserved?

4. Smedes, *Forgive and Forget*, p. 59.

5. What did David's merciful response communicate to Abishai and the nation?

6. What can you learn from David's deathbed pronouncement of judgment on Shimei?

7. Review Lewis Smedes' fable on pages 172–174. What hits closest to your heart?

# Chapter 22

# A SONG OF TRIUMPH

## 2 Samuel 22

As we enter the final phase of David's life, the long shadows of age are stretching across his rugged face. Instead of being a season of rest and reflection, however, David's twilight years bring even more storms for him to endure.

On the heels of Absalom's rebellion comes a man named Sheba from Saul's home tribe, Benjamin. Stirring up dissension, Sheba leads the northern tribes to withdraw their support from David. Only Judah remains loyal to the crown. Alarmed by the clouds of civil war gathering on the horizon, David says to his commander Amasa[1] (whom he has chosen to replace Joab): "Now Sheba the son of Bichri will do us more harm than Absalom" (2 Sam. 20:6a).

He orders Amasa to kill Sheba and douse the revolt before it flares out of control. But before Amasa can track down Sheba, Joab coldly murders him and commandeers David's troops. The disgraceful affair ends well enough, with Sheba beheaded and the uprising quelled, but David's authority is dealt a damaging blow (see vv. 7–26).

When it seems things can't get worse, they often do. In David's case, Sheba's rebellion is followed by a severe famine that strikes the land for three years (21:1). And after that, war with Philistia breaks out again (21:15). Weary from his seemingly endless struggles, David finds rest in God's faithful care and composes a triumphant song declaring God's absolute dependability in times of turmoil.

## The Prelude to the Song

David's song is recorded in two places: 2 Samuel 22 and Psalm 18. The prelude in 2 Samuel 22:1 makes clear the reason David penned his words:

> And David spoke the words of this song to the

---

1. Amasa was another of David's nephews, the son of his other sister, Abigail (see 1 Chron. 2:12–17). Amasa had also been Absalom's military commander (2 Sam. 17:25). David's choice to replace Joab with him shows David's wisdom in reuniting Israel after Absalom's death, his grace to this nephew who had served in the rebellion, and his displeasure with Joab, who had killed Absalom.

Lord in the day that the Lord delivered him from the
hand of all his enemies and from the hand of Saul.

God's faithful deliverance from his enemies provides the inspiration for David's praise. How many battles had he fought over the years? There were the wars with Philistia, Aram, and Ammon. There were enemies like Goliath, Achish, Sheba, his own son Absalom, and, of course, his fiercest adversary, Saul.

He described the storms that he endured at the hands of his foes as "waves of death" and "torrents of destruction" (v. 5), "cords of Sheol" and "snares of death" (v. 6), "distress" (v. 7), and "calamity" (v. 19). In every tempest, though, David found a shelter in the Lord.

## The Themes of the Song

As we examine David's hymn of praise, four themes of deliverance echo through the stanzas.

### When Times Are Tough, the Lord Is Our Only Security

Are you trudging through tough times? Comfort your heart with David's images of God in verses 2–4:

> "The Lord is my rock and my fortress and my
>     deliverer;
> My God, my rock, in whom I take refuge;
> My shield and the horn of my salvation, my
>     stronghold and my refuge;
> My savior, Thou dost save me from violence.
> I call upon the Lord, who is worthy to be praised;
> And I am saved from my enemies."

"Rock," "fortress," "refuge," "shield," "horn of salvation," "stronghold"—each image speaks of God's security. David found that security when, in his distress, he called to the Lord (v. 7). God heard his cry for help and came to his rescue with the power and fury of a thunderstorm:

> "Then the earth shook and quaked,
> The foundations of heaven were trembling
> And were shaken, because He was angry.
> Smoke went up out of His nostrils,
> And fire from His mouth devoured;
> Coals were kindled by it.

He bowed the heavens also, and came down
With thick darkness under His feet.
And He rode on a cherub and flew;
And He appeared on the wings of the wind.
And He made darkness canopies around Him,
A mass of waters, thick clouds of the sky.
From the brightness before Him
Coals of fire were kindled.
The Lord thundered from heaven,
And the Most High uttered His voice.
And He sent out arrows, and scattered them,
Lightning, and routed them.
Then the channels of the sea appeared,
The foundations of the world were laid bare,
By the rebuke of the Lord,
At the blast of the breath of His nostrils.
He sent from on high, He took me;
He drew me out of many waters.
He delivered me from my strong enemy,
From those who hated me, for they were too
    strong for me." (vv. 8–18)

Summing up, David wrote,

"They confronted me in the day of my calamity,
But the Lord was my support.
He also brought me forth into a broad place;
He rescued me, because He delighted in me."
(vv. 19–20)

Though your enemies deal harshly with you, the Lord will support you. What keeps His mighty arms always open, always willing
to hold you and defend you when you need Him? David gave the
answer: "He rescued me, because *He delighted in me*" (v. 20b, emphasis added). Hang on to that truth in the midst of your calamity.
Caring for you, He feels your ache. Delighting in you, He will be
your security.

### When Days Are Dark, the Lord Is Our Only Light

In his darkest times, David found a lamp to light his way:

"For Thou art my lamp, O Lord;
And the Lord illumines my darkness." (v. 29)

Carrying a lantern into a forest night doesn't guarantee you'll see all the trees. It only means that you can see a few steps ahead of you, far enough to keep your footing sure. Likewise, as the Lord lights your path, He may not shine all the answers to the shadowy questions in your mind, but He will give you all the light you need to scale life's obstacles with confidence and agility.

> "For by Thee I can run upon a troop;
> By my God I can leap over a wall." (v. 30)

David also pictured the Lord as his lamp in Psalm 27:

> The Lord is my light and my salvation;
> Whom shall I fear?
> The Lord is the defense of my life;
> Whom shall I dread? (v. 1)

Is there fear in your life? Fear of failure . . . fear of the unknown . . . fear of financial disaster . . . fear of losing someone you love? Remember, His light is yours. His Word is sure. "He is a shield to all who take refuge in Him" (2 Sam. 22:31b).

### When Our Walk Is Weak, the Lord Is Our Only Strength

David was by no means strong in himself. In fact, when he was ruled by his own passions, his seemingly solid-marble character proved to be cracked and chipped and flawed. The key to David's strength was that he acknowledged God as its source.

> "God is my strong fortress;
> And He sets the blameless in His way.
> He makes my feet like hinds' feet,
> And sets me on my high places.
> He trains my hands for battle,
> So that my arms can bend a bow of bronze.
> Thou hast also given me the shield of Thy
>     salvation,
> And Thy help makes me great."
> (vv. 33–36)

God gave David deerlike footing to scale the treacherous mountains in his life. He also provided strength to defeat those who sought to pull him down. With every Goliath David faced, God was his champion: "Thou has subdued under me those who rose up against me" (v. 40b). And when the sneering menace turned out to be his own countrymen, "Thou hast also delivered me from the contentions of my people" (v. 44a).

The Lord turned David's battlegrounds into proving grounds for his faith. For when David was at his weakest, God was at His strongest; when David was crumbling shale, God was solid granite (see also 2 Cor. 12:7–10). Reflecting on God's mighty grace, David exclaimed:

> "The Lord lives, and blessed be my rock;
> And exalted be God, the rock of my salvation."
> (2 Sam. 22:47)

### When Our Future Is Foggy, the Lord Is Our Only Hope

As David finished his song, he peered down the corridor of time to his descendants. There, in the distant future, he saw his God still protecting, still providing, still keeping the promises He made to him when he first became king (see 7:8–16):

> "Therefore I will give thanks to Thee, O Lord,
>     among the nations,
> And I will sing praises to Thy name.
> He is a tower of deliverance to His king,
> And shows lovingkindness to His anointed,
> To David and his descendants forever."
> (22:50–51)

Is your future foggy? Are you unsure of tomorrow? Parts of your future will always be a mystery to you. But there are a few things you *can* count on as God's child—eternal promises that cut through the clouds like shafts of sunlight. God's lovingkindness. The guidance of His Word. His strength when our faith is weak. And His fountain of hope when all our streams have run dry.

### A Psalm of David

> *The steps of a man are established by the Lord;*
> *And He delights in his way.*
> *When he falls, he shall not be hurled headlong;*
> *Because the Lord is the One who holds his hand.*
> *I have been young, and now I am old;*
> *Yet I have not seen the righteous forsaken,*
> *Or his descendants begging bread. . . .*
> *But the salvation of the righteous is from the Lord;*

*He is their strength in time of trouble.*
*And the Lord helps them, and delivers them;*
*He delivers them from the wicked, and saves them,*
*Because they take refuge in Him.*
(Ps. 37:23–25, 39–40)

 ## Living Insights

"The happiest place on earth." Those shimmering words, arched above the entrance to Disneyland, invite thousands of people every day to shed their troubles like heavy overcoats and escape to a land of sunshine and storybook adventures.

Our hearts long for a place like Disneyland—a place where flowers bloom year-round, dreams come true precisely on schedule, and children of all races sing "It's a Small World" in perfect harmony. Where we live, Main Street is littered with trash and lined with boarded-up windows. Disneyland's Main Street, on the other hand, offers parades and popcorn, huggable cartoon characters and horse-drawn carriage rides, sparkling lights and dazzling fireworks. What a great place to live!

Unfortunately, we can only visit Disneyland. Each night, when the park closes down, the lights go out, the music ends, and the magic melts like a half-eaten ice cream cone.

A Disneyland adventure may help us forget our problems for a while, but it doesn't solve them. Thankfully, God gives us more than a magic kingdom; His kingdom offers us solid hope for a real world. He meets us in the panic and stress of our everyday life, where the tigers are real and the roller coaster rides don't always end safely.

As you consider the four themes from our chapter, reflect on the world where you live. When are times the toughest for you?

_____

_____

When are your days the darkest?

_____

_____

When is your walk the weakest?

_____

_____

When is your future the foggiest?

_____

_____

Into your world steps God and His kingdom of love and truth. What does it mean that He is your only security?

_____

_____

When does He show you His light?

_____

_____

How does He demonstrate His power in your life?

_____

_____

How does He give you hope?

_____

_____

God has the strength to deliver us from any problem. And sometimes, he does. But He didn't promise to take away every problem—not in this life, anyway. Rather, He promised to take us _through_ them. He offers security, light, power, and hope. Real help for a real world.

# Questions for Group Discussion

1. "Enemies fall into these categories: those who have hurt us directly, those who threaten to hurt us . . . those who disagree with us."[2] In which category do most of your enemies fit?

2. David's enemies mainly fell into the first two categories. His problem wasn't how to get along with disagreeable people as much as how to avoid being killed. Few of us have enemies with murder on their minds, yet sometimes an enemy will stick an emotional knife in our back. Have you ever had an enemy like that?

3. When threatened, what was David's response (see 2 Samuel 22:2–7)? What is your typical response?

4. It's natural to be afraid of an enemy's strength. However, an enemy's power pales in comparison to God's power. Read verses 8–18. How does God demonstrate His strength today? How does this calm your fears?

5. What confidence does verse 20 give you?

6. Take a moment to review the four themes we found in David's psalm. What supports does God offer you as you face the threat of an enemy?

7. In what ways can you rely on these supports this week?

2. Gary Richmond, from the sermon "Life Is a Zoo," given at the First Evangelical Free Church of Fullerton, California, January 30, 1994.

## Chapter 23

# WHEN THE GODLY ARE FOOLISH

### 2 Samuel 24; 1 Chronicles 21

**M**ost children outgrow their childish ways. As they mature, they shed the name-calling, the my-dad-is-bigger-than-your-dad mentality, the steady diet of candy and gum.

But sadly, as God's children we never outgrow our worst habit: sin. We are never immune from its appeal. In fact, those who fall the hardest are often those who have walked the longest with God. And when spiritual leaders fall, they usually take a host of innocent people with them.

In this chapter, we see David—worn with age and gray at his temples—make a foolish decision based on pride. The consequences of his choice are staggering, and they remind us all of the seriousness of sin.

## Analysis of the Decision

David's fateful decision came on the heels of Israel's latest war with the Philistines. David and his valiant men had cut down four giants—one of whom had twelve fingers and twelve toes (see 1 Chron. 20). Fresh from victory, David was vulnerable once again.

### David's Motive

In 2 Samuel 24:2, David commanded Joab to take a census of the people. Now there was nothing evil about taking a census. The Lord Himself had ordered Moses to count the people at the beginning and end of their forty years of wandering in the wilderness (see Num. 1:1–3; 26:1–4). But what motivated David was not obedience to God but pride in his own power. By counting the people, he was calculating the potential strength of his army and, in effect, slighting the faithfulness of God as the shield of Israel (compare Ps. 89:17–18). David's census "represented an unwarranted glorying in and dependence on human power rather than the Lord."[1]

---

1. J. Robert Vannoy, note on 2 Samuel 24:1, in *The NIV Study Bible*, ed. Kenneth L. Barker and others (Grand Rapids, Mich.: Zondervan Bible Publishers, 1985), p. 461.

Joab could see through David's sinful purpose and questioned him openly.

> "Now may the Lord your God add to the people a hundred times as many as they are, while the eyes of my lord the king still see; but why does my lord the king delight in this thing?" (2 Sam. 24:3)

But David was determined.

> Nevertheless, the king's word prevailed against Joab and against the commanders of the army. So Joab and the commanders of the army went out from the presence of the king, to register the people of Israel. (v. 4)

David's decision reveals two things about his personal life at this time. First, *he was out of touch with the Lord*. We don't read of prayer, of seeking God's counsel, of consulting one of God's prophets for help in his decision. He simply decided to do it. Second, *he was unaccountable to anyone around him*. By dismissing Joab, apparently not even answering his question, the mighty king of Israel showed that he thought he answered to nobody.

### God's Purpose

There was more, however, to David's decision than his pride. Backing up to verse 1, we see the Lord working behind the scenes:

> Now again the anger of the Lord burned against Israel, and it incited David against them to say, "Go, number Israel and Judah." (v. 1)

The divine purpose for the census was judgment, perhaps because Israel had abandoned David, the Lord's anointed, by following the rebels Absalom and Sheba.[2] Interestingly, in the parallel account in 1 Chronicles, Satan—not the Lord—is the instigator:

> Then Satan stood up against Israel and moved David to number Israel.[3] (1 Chron. 21:1)

How can we reconcile these accounts? Was the root of David's decision his pride, the Lord's anger, or Satan's hatefulness? The

2. Vannoy, note on 2 Samuel 24:1, in *The NIV Study Bible*, p. 461.

3. The Hebrew word for *moved* in 1 Chronicles 21:1 is the same for *incited* in 2 Samuel 24:1: *suth*.

answer is . . . yes to all three, because all three played a role in the decision.

As part of God's judgment, the Lord allowed Satan to tempt David (for God cannot tempt anyone; see James 1:13).[4] Determined to do as much damage as he could, Satan found a crack of pride in David's character and moved him to lead the nation into destruction.

However, what Satan planned for evil, God would use for good. Satan expected the divine judgment to crush David, but God would use it to refine him. And the sword of justice that Satan hoped would wipe out the nation, God would use to demonstrate His mercy to the world.

## Impact of the Decision

With a heavy heart, Joab obeyed David's ill-advised command to count the people. For more than nine months, Joab and his men traveled the land collecting data (2 Sam. 24:5–8).[5] Finally, with their books lined with rows of numbers, they returned with the results:

> And Joab gave the number of the registration of the people to the king; and there were in Israel eight hundred thousand valiant men who drew the sword, and the men of Judah were five hundred thousand men. (v. 9)

### A Troubled Conscience

Any king would have been elated over these figures. For David, however, they added up to one glaring reality: his lack of trust in God. As a result,

> David's heart troubled him after he had numbered the people. (v. 10a)

In Hebrew, *troubled* means "to attack or to smite." The word is used in both senses in 1 Samuel 17:34–35, in which David "attacked"

4. Scripture contains many examples of God and Satan involved in the same event but with opposite motives: the sufferings of Job (Job 1–2), the persecution of Christians (1 Pet. 4:13–19; 5:8), the sifting of Peter (Luke 22:31–32), and the crucifixion of Christ. For further explanation, see *Encyclopedia of Bible Difficulties*, by Gleason L. Archer (Grand Rapids, Mich.: Zondervan Publishing House, Regency Reference Library, 1982), pp. 186–88.

5. According to 1 Chronicles 21:6, Joab refused to include the tribes of Levi and Benjamin in the census, perhaps to keep the worship of God from being tainted by David's sin. Levi was the priestly tribe, and the tabernacle and the ark were located within the borders of Benjamin. See Raymond Dillard, notes on 1 Chronicles 21:6, in *The NIV Study Bible*, p. 612.

a lion or a bear that endangered his flock and "struck him." Later in the account, David slung a stone at Goliath and "struck the Philistine" (v. 50). Now, years later, David was the one endangering the sheep of Israel, and his conscience struck him with grief.

Tormented by his sin, David finally cast aside his pride and flew to God in humble confession.

> So David said to the Lord, "I have sinned greatly in what I have done. But now, O Lord, please take away the iniquity of Thy servant, for I have acted very foolishly." (2 Sam. 24:10b)

The mark of a person after God's heart is not perfection but a sensitivity to sin and a willingness to seek restoration with God, even if it means facing His judgment.

### A Hard Choice to Make

To reinforce the painful lesson about responsibility, God let David choose his own consequences—perhaps the most severe punishment of all. According to the account in 1 Chronicles,

> And the Lord spoke to Gad, David's seer, saying, "Go and speak to David, saying, 'Thus says the Lord, "I offer you three things; choose for yourself one of them, that I may do it to you."'" So Gad came to David and said to him, "Thus says the Lord, 'Take for yourself either three years of famine, or three months to be swept away before your foes, while the sword of your enemies overtakes you, or else three days of the sword of the Lord, even pestilence in the land, and the angel of the Lord destroying throughout all the territory of Israel.' Now, therefore, consider what answer I shall return to Him who sent me." (21:9–12)

The grim ramifications of his choice bound David in a horrible dilemma. He cried out to the prophet Gad, "I am in great distress" (v. 13a). Wisely, he chose the third option, for even under judgment, a person is safest within the hand of God.

> "Please let me fall into the hand of the Lord, for His mercies are very great. But do not let me fall into the hand of man." (v. 13b)

### A Consequence to Bear

God's judgment was swift and terrible: "So the Lord sent a pestilence on Israel; 70,000 men of Israel fell" (v. 14). But equally swift was His mercy.

> And God sent an angel to Jerusalem to destroy it; but as he was about to destroy it, the Lord saw and was sorry over the calamity, and said to the destroying angel, "It is enough; now relax your hand." And the angel of the Lord was standing by the threshing floor of Ornan the Jebusite. (v. 15)

When David saw the angel wielding his sword over Jerusalem, he fell on his face before God and shifted the full weight of blame upon himself:

> "Is it not I who commanded to count the people? Indeed, I am the one who has sinned and done very wickedly, but these sheep, what have they done? O Lord my God, please let Thy hand be against me and my father's household, but not against Thy people that they should be plagued." (v. 17)

## Altar and Deliverance

God could have ordered the angel to bring down his sword of justice on David's neck. Instead, He gave him another message through the prophet Gad.

### Command and Provision

At the site where God's judgment and mercy met, David was to

> go up and build an altar to the Lord on the threshing floor of Ornan the Jebusite. (v. 18)

Although Ornan was not a Jew, he owned a piece of property that was precious to all Jews. Overlooking the city of David, this hill was where the angel restrained Abraham's hand from plunging a knife into his son Isaac and where God provided a lamb as substitute (see Gen. 22:9–14). Here on Mount Moriah, God would once again hold back the hand of death and provide salvation for His people.

### Offer and Response

Renewed with hope, David hurried to see Ornan, who bowed his face before the king.

> Then David said to Ornan, "Give me the site of this threshing floor, that I may build on it an altar to the Lord; for the full price you shall give it to me, that the plague may be restrained from the people." (1 Chron. 21:22)

Ornan generously offered to give David not only the threshing floor but also

> "the oxen for burnt offerings and the threshing sledges for wood and the wheat for the grain offering; I will give it all." (v. 23b)

But David refused the gift:

> "No, but I will surely buy it for the full price; for I will not take what is yours for the Lord, or offer a burnt offering which costs me nothing." So David gave Ornan 600 shekels of gold by weight for the site. (vv. 24–25)

### Construction and Relief

The Lord honored David's zeal. When David built the altar and called to the Lord for mercy, a blast of fire answered from heaven and consumed the sacrifice (v. 26). His holy wrath appeased,

> the Lord commanded the angel, and he put his sword back in its sheath. (v. 27)

### Worship and Vow

Trembling and worshiping at the foot of the smoking altar, David understood God's grace more clearly now than at any other time in his life. The story ends as he makes a solemn vow:

> "This is the house of the Lord God, and this is the altar of burnt offering for Israel." (22:1)

This is the place, David is saying, where God's judgment and mercy will meet for generations to come, where sins will be atoned for and pardon be bestowed. To this holy mountain the world would come to find mercy . . . and hope . . . and salvation. For here Solomon would build the temple of the Lord.

## Three Practical Suggestions

David learned many never-to-be-forgotten lessons that day—lessons about the devastation of sin, the holiness of God, the hope of the altar, and the need for grace. He also learned that nobody—no matter how old, how wise, how respected—is immune to sin. How can we keep from making foolish decisions that damage our lives and those around us? Here are a few suggestions.

First, *be accountable*. To live an unaccountable life is to invite danger. Second, *remember sin's consequences*. Keep the seventy thousand Israelite graves fresh in your mind.[6] Third, *take God seriously*. Failing to do so is to deny His lordship in our lives.

It's true. We will never outgrow sin altogether, but by God's grace, we can learn to hate it more deeply and to see it less frequently in our lives.

### A Psalm of David

*O Lord, I call upon Thee; hasten to me!*
*Give ear to my voice when I call to Thee!*
*May my prayer be counted as incense before Thee;*
*The lifting up of my hands as the evening offering.*
*Set a guard, O Lord, over my mouth;*
*Keep watch over the door of my lips.*
*Do not incline my heart to any evil thing,*
*To practice deeds of wickedness. . . .*
*Let the righteous smite me in kindness and reprove me;*
*It is oil upon the head;*
*Do not let my head refuse it.*
(Ps. 141:1–4a, 5a)

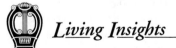 *Living Insights*

This story from David's life provides one of the most dramatic pictures of salvation in the Bible. The angel of the Lord appears

---

6. Scripture says that "70,000 men of Israel fell" (1 Chron. 21:14). The total number of deaths may have been much higher if women and children had been counted.

191

with his terrible sword of justice drawn and ready to strike the condemned. But between the angel and the sinners is an altar, and on the altar is a sacrifice. A humble prayer is spoken, and the sky unleashes a thunderbolt of fire—the wrath of God—that consumes not the sinners but the sacrifice. Justice served, the angel sheathes his sword, and the sinners are set free.

Upon this hill of mercy, known as Mount Moriah, the foundation is laid for the temple and its sacrifices—as well as the redemption of the world.

For we are the condemned sinners standing beneath the angel's blade on a hill called Mount Calvary. The altar is the cross. And the sacrifice is Christ.

The apostle Paul fits these pieces together in his definitive statement of salvation truth:

> But God demonstrates His own love toward us, in that while we were yet sinners, Christ died for us. Much more then, having now been justified by His blood, we shall be saved from the wrath of God through Him. (Rom. 5:8–9)

Christ's sacrifice frees us from God's wrath. Why, then, do we often live in fear of it?

Christ's death covers all our sins, even the ones that have left a trail of destruction in their path. The abortion. The affair. The rebellion. How long will we condemn ourselves for the sins God has forgiven?

God has sheathed His sword. Maybe it's time to put ours away too.

## Questions for Group Discussion

1. David's purpose for taking the census was to glory in his own strength rather than in the Lord's protection. In a sense, he was saying, "I don't need God; I'm strong enough to take care of myself and determine my own destiny." You may never come out and say that, but do your actions ever communicate it? In what ways?

2. According to Proverb 16:5a, "Everyone who is proud in heart is an abomination to the Lord." Strong words. Why do you think God hates pride so much?

3. Why was it hard for David to feel happy about the results of his census? He got what he wanted, didn't he? Have you ever felt like him?

4. How did David's choice of consequences reveal his change of heart toward God?

5. The three consequences presented David with an agonizing dilemma. But God faced a dilemma too. How could He pardon David's sin and the sins of Israel without compromising His holiness? How did God solve that dilemma at the threshing floor of Ornan?

6. How did He solve that dilemma for us at the Cross?

## Chapter 24

# THE END OF AN ERA

*1 Chronicles 28–29*

A sculpture is only as good as the quality of the marble. That's why the best artists insist on handpicking their stone. They know what they're looking for—the color, the grain, the texture, and whether there are any impurities that would cause the marble to crumble under the hammer and chisel.

David was once an unhewn stone in the vast quarry of Judah. But the Master Artist saw in him the qualities He needed to produce one of His finest works of art. So He chose David out of the pit and began sculpting him into an enduring masterpiece.

Now, more than fifty years later, God's work is nearly finished. With a hand that has seemed severe at times, God has chiseled the hard edges of David's life and filed the rough spots. He has done this not to break David, but to bring out his innate qualities—his spirituality, humility, and integrity—and, ultimately, to magnify His name.

We observed David's qualities in raw form in chapter 1 of our study. In this final chapter, we'll see them polished and honed, as David focuses on four activities before his life draws to a close.

## Reflecting on the Temple

Realizing his end is near, David has called together an august assembly of national leaders, including Solomon, the king-elect, to deliver his final farewell. These are the knights of David's round table—his princes, commanders, and mighty men, some of whom have served him from the beginning (1 Chron. 28:1).

As the aging warrior slowly rises to his feet, the room fills with an air of respect and loving admiration. What is foremost on David's mind at this epochal moment? The great battles or accomplishments of the past? No, David's thoughts are on worship and the future building of the temple.

> "Listen to me, my brethren and my people; I had intended to build a permanent home for the ark of the covenant of the Lord and for the footstool of our God. So I had made preparations to build it. But God said to me, 'You shall not build a house for My

name because you are a man of war and have shed blood.'" (vv. 2–3)

Yet, even though the Lord barred David from fulfilling his cherished dream, He had chosen him "to be king over Israel forever"—a reference to the Davidic covenant and God's promise of an enduring dynasty (v. 4). And He has now chosen his son, Solomon, to build his temple and inherit the blessing (vv. 6–7).

Rather than pining over what he couldn't do, David overflows with gratitude for what God has given him—a noble son who will live out his legacy. Every parent should be so honored! David's advice to his followers is this:

> "So now, in the sight of all Israel, the assembly of the Lord, and in the hearing of our God, observe and seek after all the commandments of the Lord your God in order that you may possess the good land and bequeath it to your sons after you forever." (v. 8)

## Speaking to His Son

Then David turns to his beloved son of grace, Solomon, whom the Lord gave him from his marriage to Bathsheba. In an emotional moment, his eyes meet Solomon's, and he offers him some final words of wisdom.

### Regarding Godliness

What would you say to your son or daughter at a time like this? As we might expect, David counsels his son about having a heart for God.

His first piece of advice is *know the Lord*.

> "As for you, my son Solomon, know the God of your father." (v. 9a)

David understands the tyranny of the urgent that pulls a leader's eyes off the truly important. He has lived with the pressures and demands of ruling a nation, and he tells his soon-to-be-king son that the greatest investment of time and energy he can make is in knowing God (see Phil. 3:10).

Next, David encourages his son to turn his knowledge into action: *serve the Lord*.

> "And serve Him with a whole heart and a willing

mind; for the Lord searches all hearts, and understands every intent of the thoughts." (1 Chron. 28:9b)

God can tell whether we're serving Him out of devotion or duty. So David warns Solomon, "Don't just go through the religious motions; put your hand *and* your heart to the task."

David's advice emerges out of a lifetime of modeling. Solomon has sung his father's psalms; he has heard his ardent prayers. He knows what wholehearted devotion looks like from watching his father. Now it's time to follow in his footsteps.

Finally, David urges his son to *seek the Lord,* to be sensitive to Him, to listen to the nudging of His voice.

> "If you seek Him, He will let you find Him; but if you forsake Him, He will reject you forever." (v. 9c)

The opposite of seeking God is ignoring Him, living as if He didn't matter, neglecting to take His commands seriously. "Don't drift aimlessly," David says. "Set your compass on God, and aggressively, decisively live each day to honor Him."

### Regarding Construction

Having said all this, David issues a charge to Solomon:

> "Consider now, for the Lord has chosen you to build a house for the sanctuary; be courageous and act." (v. 10)

Then he excitedly unrolls the temple blueprints. David's eyes gleam as he tours Solomon through each room, from the storehouses to the chamber where God's glory will dwell. Then, with a fine brush, he paints every detail for his son: the size of the rooms, the weight of the utensils, even the divisions and duties of the priests (vv. 11–18).

Along with information, David pours into his son's soul a passion for God. As he hands over the blueprints, David points to the source of the vision that he is entrusting to Solomon:

> "All this," said David, "the Lord made me understand in writing by His hand upon me, all the details of this pattern." (v. 19)

### Regarding Ruling

Building this magnificent structure while ruling a nation will not be easy. At times, Solomon will feel overwhelmed. So David's final word to his son is an encouragement that God will be with him, as will the priests.

> "Be strong and courageous, and act; do not fear nor be dismayed, for the Lord God, my God, is with you. He will not fail you nor forsake you until all the work for the service of the house of the Lord is finished. Now behold, there are the divisions of the priests and the Levites for all the service of the house of God, and every willing man of any skill will be with you in all the work for all kinds of service. The officials also and all the people will be entirely at your command." (vv. 20–21)

But will the people get behind this costly temple project, particularly when the bills start coming due?

David turns to the assembly and challenges them to make a donation to the temple by his example of offering his own treasure:

> "In my delight in the house of my God, the treasure I have of gold and silver, I give to the house of my God, over and above all that I have already provided for the holy temple. . . . Who then is willing to consecrate himself this day to the Lord?" (29:3, 5b)

Enthusiasm electrifies the hall as one person after another pledges gold, silver, and precious stones to the temple. Each gift is offered willingly "to the Lord with a whole heart" (v. 9).

## Praying from His Heart

David's joy can hardly be contained as he sees the fire of his vision ablaze in the hearts of his subjects. He lifts his voice toward heaven in one of the richest prayers in the Bible.

### Praise

The first words to pour out of his mouth are praise to God as the supreme King and Benefactor of Israel.

> "Blessed art Thou, O Lord God of Israel our father, forever and ever. Thine, O Lord, is the greatness and the power and the glory and the victory and the majesty, indeed everything that is in the heavens and the earth; Thine is the dominion, O Lord, and

Thou dost exalt Thyself as head over all. Both riches and honor come from Thee, and Thou dost rule over all, and in Thy hand is power and might; and it lies in Thy hand to make great, and to strengthen everyone." (vv. 10–12)

### Thanksgiving

David looks at himself in light of God's glory, amazed that God accepts his offering. His heart overflows with humble gratitude.

"Who am I and who are my people that we should be able to offer as generously as this? For all things come from Thee, and from Thy hand we have given Thee. For we are sojourners before Thee, and tenants, as all our fathers were; our days on the earth are like a shadow, and there is no hope. O Lord our God, all this abundance that we have provided to build Thee a house for Thy holy name, it is from Thy hand, and all is Thine." (vv. 14–16)

David's scale of values is perfectly balanced. He knows that his palace, his riches, his throne—everything he owns—belongs to God, who can take it from his hand at any time. The closer David comes to the portal of death, the more clearly he sees that life is little more than a wisp of air, a passing shadow. Yet it is not without meaning, because God has given him the privilege of building a legacy of worship and praise that will endure for generations.

### Intercession

Then He prays for his people, particularly for Solomon, that they will endeavor to follow the Lord as he has done:

"O Lord, the God of Abraham, Isaac, and Israel, our fathers, preserve this forever in the intentions of the heart of Thy people, and direct their heart to Thee; and give to my son Solomon a perfect heart to keep Thy commandments, Thy testimonies, and Thy statutes, and to do them all, and to build the temple, for which I have made provision." (vv. 18–19)

## Rejoicing of the Assembly

In a climactic and fitting finish to David's life, the entire assembly bows in homage to the Lord first, and then to him (v. 20). A time of celebration follows, with everyone eating and drinking "before the Lord with great gladness" (v. 22). Solomon is anointed king, and all the officials and mighty men swear their allegiance to him.

How many more days David lived is hard to say. When the Holy Spirit shines the light back on David, we see that his lamp is dim. The king's life light, once a blazing fire, fades and flickers like a candle in the wind . . . then goes out.

> Then he died in a ripe old age, full of days, riches and honor. (v. 28a)

With David's death comes the end of an era. For as great a ruler as Solomon became, he never quite achieved the stature of his father. The chronicles of David's "reign, his power . . . on Israel, and on all the kingdoms of the lands" (v. 30) are preserved for us forever so that we can emulate the heart God called His own.

### A Psalm of David

*I will extol Thee, my God, O King;*
*And I will bless Thy name forever and ever.*
*Every day I will bless Thee,*
*And I will praise Thy name forever and ever.*
*Great is the Lord, and highly to be praised;*
*And His greatness is unsearchable.*
*One generation shall praise Thy works to another,*
*And shall declare Thy mighty acts.*
*On the glorious splendor of Thy majesty,*
*And on Thy wonderful works, I will meditate.*
*And men shall speak of the power of Thine awesome*
*    acts;*
*And I will tell of Thy greatness.*
*They shall eagerly utter the memory of Thine*
*    abundant goodness,*
*And shall shout joyfully of Thy righteousness.*

*The Lord is gracious and merciful;*
*Slow to anger and great in lovingkindness.*
*The Lord is good to all,*
*And His mercies are over all His works.*

*All Thy works shall give thanks to Thee, O Lord,*
*And Thy godly ones shall bless Thee.*
*They shall speak of the glory of Thy kingdom,*
*And talk of Thy power;*
*To make known to the sons of men Thy mighty acts,*
*And the glory of the majesty of Thy kingdom.*
*Thy kingdom is an everlasting kingdom,*
*And Thy dominion endures throughout all*
*    generations.* (Ps. 145:1–13)

 *Living Insights*

Imagine strolling through the stately Galleria dell' Accademia in Florence, Italy. You enter a magnificent room with an arching ceiling, and there stands Michelangelo's statue, the *David*.

The powerful figure's lifelikeness immediately strikes you. The chest seems to rise with a breath of air; the shoulder muscles, to tighten and relax; the head, to turn. The longer you examine the figure, the more you admire it . . . and the artist who created it.

The same is true with the real David. We marvel at David's courage in battle and his ability to inspire others. But if we stop there, we miss the point of his life, which was to glorify His Creator.

He glorified God through his humble admission of sin, his passion for worship, his preparations to build the temple, his grateful attitude, his beautiful psalms, and his undying devotion.

In all these ways and more, David expressed the Master's handiwork in his life.

God hasn't set aside his hammer and chisel, you know. He's still creating masterpieces from the raw material we bring him. Are you willing to let Him shape and file you into a beautiful work of art?

What area of your life might you need to surrender to God's will?

_____

_____

_____

What's one way you can deepen your devotion to Him?

_____

_____

_____

_____

What single principle have you learned from David's life that you can take with you as you close this study?

_____

_____

_____

If David could speak, his parting words of wisdom to us would probably be the same as those he offered Solomon: know the Lord, serve the Lord, seek the Lord.

 *Questions for Group Discussion*

1. Perhaps more than any other person in the Old Testament, David lived out the command, "And you shall love the Lord your God with all your heart and with all your soul and with all your might" (Deut. 6:5). How did David express his love for God as he neared the end of his life?

2. David was passing his crown to his son, but what else of more lasting value was he handing down to Solomon?

3. As we approach death, the things that used to seem important aren't as important anymore. Review David's prayer in 1 Chronicles 29:13–16. What was his perspective on material things?

4. As a father, David was primarily concerned about his son's heart (see 28:9; 29:19). As long as Solomon had a strong relationship with God, David knew his son could deal with the other issues of his life. How can you help your children develop a heart for God? (If you don't have children, consider your nephews or nieces, or children in your church.)

5. Finish this statement: "The most significant lesson that God has taught me through the life of David is _____."

# BOOKS FOR
# PROBING FURTHER

David was paradox personified.

He slew Goliath with the fling of a stone, but he was wounded by the lust of his own wandering eyes. He soothed Saul's spirit with the soft strains of his harp, but he exploded in anger at Nabal. He offered Jonathan's crippled son, Mephibosheth, a seat at his royal table, but ignored the needs of his own children. He hid from God after his affair with Bathsheba . . . but, oh, he knew how to draw near.

How could such an inconsistent man be considered someone after God's own heart? David's heart beat with God's not because he was perfect, but because he was *devoted*. One passion was greater than all the others: his desire to know and obey God.

We hope this study of David's life has compelled you to put your ears to God's Word and listen for His heartbeat—so that yours will begin to pulse with it. The following books will help you in your pursuit.

Foster, Richard J. *Prayer: Finding the Heart's True Home*. San Francisco, Calif.: Harper San Francisco, 1992. If devotion to God is a fire within the soul, prayer is the billows that keeps the embers glowing. This book examines prayer from three angles: prayers that draw us inward for personal transformation, prayers that lift us upward toward intimacy with God, and prayers that lead us outward in ministry.

Inrig, Gary. *Quality Friendship*. Chicago, Ill.: Moody Press, 1981. The best example of biblical friendship is found in David's relationship with Jonathan. In this book, the author uses David and Jonathan to model the type of friendships all of us should build— friendships based on loyalty, commitment, and a deep love.

Keller, W. Phillip. *David: The Time of Saul's Tyranny*. Waco, Tex.: Word Books, 1985. *David: The Shepherd King*. Waco, Tex.: Word Books, 1986. In these two volumes, the author blends keen scholarship with a sensitive, devotional style. Familiarizing you with the life of this godly yet very human man, Keller paints these portraits of David's life with dramatic colors and confronts you with a stark call to obedience.

Smedes, Lewis B. *Forgive and Forget: Healing the Hurts We Don't Deserve*. San Francisco, Calif.: Harper and Row, Publishers, 1984. This book is about being free. It explains not only *why* you need to be free from the hurts that embitter and bind you but *how* you can be free. And Smedes's honest approach is liberating as well. He expects no perfection, induces no guilt. He only encourages us to take steps toward being forgivers.

Sproul, R. C. *The Soul's Quest for God*. Wheaton, Ill.: Tyndale House Publishers, 1992. Our souls are hungry for deeper, more intimate knowledge of God, but where do we begin? This book points us in the right direction—to the Scriptures—and helps us understand how the Holy Spirit feeds our souls as we meet God in His Word.

Swindoll, Charles R. *Killing Giants, Pulling Thorns*. Grand Rapids, Mich.: Zondervan Publishing House, 1994. The practical and biblical principles in this book help you face the giants that threaten your spiritual life.

White, John. *Parents in Pain*. Downers Grove, Ill.: InterVarsity Press, 1979. If you found yourself relating to David in the midst of his domestic whirlwind, you'll find help in this book. Compassionately, the author discusses feelings of guilt, frustration, anger, and inadequacy that parents experience when their children wrestle with problems like alcoholism, homosexuality, and suicide. Rich in both counsel and comfort, this book will help calm the storm in your home.

Whitney, Donald S. *Spiritual Disciplines for the Christian Life*. Colorado Springs, Colo.: NavPress, 1991. David often found God in the night watches, when he and the Lord walked together in quiet communion. Would you like to enrich your experiences with God? This book is a practical manual for God-seekers who need help in the spiritual disciplines of Bible meditation, prayer, worship, journaling, and more.

Wilkes, Peter. *Overcoming Anger and Other Dragons of the Soul: Shaking Loose from Persistent Sins*. Downers Grove, Ill.: InterVarsity Press, 1987. Anger . . . lust . . . pride: "dragons of the soul." David knew them, deep in the hidden darkness of his heart.

What about you? In this book, the author shows us how to loose ourselves from the shackles of those persistent sins that imprison us.

Some of these books may be out of print and available only through a library. For those currently available, please contact your local Christian bookstore. Books by Charles R. Swindoll may be obtained through Insight for Living. IFL also offers some books by other authors—please note the ordering information that follows and contact the office that serves you.

# NOTES

# NOTES

# NOTES

# NOTES

# NOTES

# ORDERING INFORMATION

## DAVID: A MAN OF PASSION AND DESTINY

If you would like to order additional Bible study guides, purchase the audiocassette series that accompanies this guide, or request our product catalogs, please contact the office that serves you.

**United States and International locations:**

Insight for Living
Post Office Box 269000
Plano, Texas 75026-9000

1-800-772-8888, 24 hours a day, seven days a week (U.S. contacts)
International constituents may contact the U.S. office through mail queries.

**Canada:**

Insight for Living Ministries
Post Office Box 2510
Vancouver, BC V6B 3W7

1-800-663-7639, 24 hours a day, seven days a week
insight.canada@insight.org

**Australia:**

Insight for Living, Inc.
20 Albert Street
Blackburn, VIC 3130, Australia

Toll-free 1800 772 888 or (03) 9877-4277, 9:00 A.M. to 5:00 P.M., Monday to Friday
iflaus@insight.org

**Internet:**

www.insight.org

### Bible Study Guide Subscription Program

Bible study guide subscriptions are available. Please call or write the office nearest you to find out how you can receive our Bible study guides on a regular basis.